Benjamin Disraeli

**Memorials of Lord Beaconsfield**

Benjamin Disraeli
**Memorials of Lord Beaconsfield**
ISBN/EAN: 9783743344167

Manufactured in Europe, USA, Canada, Australia, Japa

Cover: Foto ©ninafisch / pixelio.de

Manufactured and distributed by brebook publishing software (www.brebook.com)

Benjamin Disraeli

**Memorials of Lord Beaconsfield**

# MEMORIALS

OF

# LORD BEACONSFIELD.

Reprinted from "The Standard."

WITH A PORTRAIT.

London:
MACMILLAN AND CO.
1881.

LONDON :
R. CLAY, SONS, AND TAYLOR,
BREAD STREET HILL.

# PREFACE.

This volume is published in response to the wish expressed by innumerable Correspondents, that not only the Biographical Notice of Lord Beaconsfield, which appeared in *The Standard* of April the 20th, but selections from the various other articles and reports published in that journal, during his last illness, death, and funeral, should be preserved for public use in an enduring shape. The following pages are a record of what occurred from the day on which Lord Beaconsfield became seriously ill to the day on which he was buried. Their contents are exclusively taken from the columns of *The Standard*. They are indeed only a selection from what was originally published in the columns of that newspaper, but nothing has been added from any other source.

# CONTENTS.

## I.
MEMOIR . . . . . . . . . . . . 1

## II.
THE LAST ILLNESS . . . . . . . . . . 83

## III.
IMPRESSIONS PRODUCED BY DEATH . . . . . . 128

## IV.
THE FUNERAL . . . . . . . . . . . 178

## V.
LORD BEACONSFIELD'S WILL . . . . . . . . 213

## VI.
SUPPLEMENTARY . . . . . . . . . . 219

APPENDIX . . . . . . . . . . . 227

# MEMORIALS

OF

# LORD BEACONSFIELD.

## I.

### MEMOIR.

LORD BEACONSFIELD was, it is generally believed, born in Bloomsbury-square, in the year 1804. His father was that Isaac Disraeli who, as author of the *Curiosities of Literature*, is familiar to all lovers of quaint learning and graceful humour. The elder Disraeli sprang from a Jewish family of the purest, or Sephardim race, that, namely, which has never left the shores of the Mediterranean. His father, who was the son of a Venetian merchant, settled in England in 1748, where he lived for nearly seventy years, and died in 1817 at the age of ninety. Isaac was born in 1766; he married in 1802 Miss Basevi, by whom he had four children, and died at Bradenham in 1848. Influenced, doubtless, to some extent by the example of his father, and being, as he was fond of saying, "born in a library," Mr. Disraeli at his first entry into life seemed inclined to make a profession of literature, having very soon abandoned the law, to which he was at first apprenticed.

A considerable interval, however, elapsed between the publication of *Vivian Grey*, that most brilliant of all maiden performances, and the author's resumption of his pen, during which Mr. Disraeli visited most of the spots famous either for natural beauty or historical associations in Europe and the Levant. But with the General Election which followed the passing of the Reform Bill began the political career which, lasting almost exactly half a century, forms one of the most remarkable phenomena of our own times. In the autumn of 1832 he issued an address to the electors of High Wycombe, and was supported at first by a combination of Radicals and Tories against the Whig candidate, but the former party deserted him at the poll, and he was defeated by a small majority. He subsequently issued an address to the electors of Marylebone, on the same principles; but the expected vacancy not occurring, he was a second time disappointed of his object. In the autumn of 1834 the Melbourne Ministry was dismissed; and Mr. Disraeli again sent out an address to the electors of High

Wycombe. It was published afterwards with the title of *The Present Crisis Examined*, and shows his mind in a transitional state. Mr. Greville, in his diary under the date 5th December, 1834, speaking of a call made upon him by the Chancellor, Lord Lyndhurst, about getting "young Disraeli" into Parliament, remarks, "his political principles must be in abeyance."

But by the spring of 1835 he had come to a definite conclusion, and at the General Election in April contested the borough of Taunton on Conservative principles. He was again defeated, and in the same year he published his *Vindication of the British Constitution*, addressed to Lord Lyndhurst, who was a warm admirer of the young and original politician, and in this essay he broached all those ideas on the subject of English history which were afterwards more fully developed in *Coningsby* and *Sybil*. In 1836 he brought out his letters of *Runnymede*, a series of attacks on the administration of Lord Melbourne. In the summer of 1837 the King died, and at the ensuing General Election Mr. Disraeli was returned for Maidstone. One story of the way in which he obtained the seat has been told as follows, but we do not pretend to vouch for it. At the General Election in 1835 Mr. Wyndham Lewis was the Conservative candidate, and according to the practice of the day, bribery and promises of bribery were rife on all sides. Mr. Lewis was beaten;

but, notwithstanding his defeat, he fulfilled all his engagements to the letter. This, and some causes of dissatisfaction with the successful candidates, rendered Mr. Lewis so popular in the borough that when, two years afterwards, the King's death caused another General Election, the party felt that they were strong enough in Maidstone not only to return Mr. Lewis, but also a Conservative colleague. Mr. Disraeli was waited upon and consented to stand, and in due course was returned. The event was important to him in more ways than one. It provided him with a seat. It secured for him the friendship of Mr. Lewis ; and when Mr. Lewis died some short time afterwards it provided for him, in the person of Mrs. Lewis, a wife who, in the words of Lord Lytton, could both console and exalt, and to whom Mr. Disraeli on more than one public occasion gratefully and affectionately referred as the solace and sweetener of his life.

There were many young men who, like him, then entered the House of Commons for the first time; but there were probably few of them concerning whom so much curiosity was excited; for the junior member for Maidstone was already a remarkable man. He was not only the author of several brilliant and popular works, but he had already taken an active part in politics. He had been a candidate for several boroughs, and in his speeches he had expressed himself freely on public men and public measures. He had nearly fought a duel with O'Connell, and had told Lord Melbourne, who asked him good-naturedly at a party whether he could be of any service to him, that he "wanted to be Prime Minister," and in the *Runnymede* letters he had singled out as the objects of his attack the most prominent members of the Ministerial body. His hatred was repaid with interest by the whole Whig Party, while the Tories, among whom he took his seat, were somewhat doubtful of the character of their new ally.

It is not wonderful, therefore, that when he rose to make his maiden speech he had few friends to back him, and received from the House at large less than the usual amount of that courtesy which is shown to a new member. No doubt he flew at high game. It was a daring thing for a new member to reply, in his maiden speech, to the great Liberator, and to include the whole Whig Party in the attack. The Whigs resolved to crush the audacious assailant, and groans, hootings, and scornful laughter arose on all sides. Mr. Disraeli attempted for some time to make head against the torrent; but, finding his efforts fruitless, he sat down with these memorable words, "I am not at all surprised at the reception I have experienced. I have begun several times many things, and I have often succeeded at last. I will sit down now, but the time will come when you will hear me." Renewed derision greeted these words, which were then supposed to be the outburst only of mortified vanity; but which time has since shown to have been the prophecy of conscious genius.

This rough reception did not daunt him from presenting himself again to his audience even in the course of the same Session. But he fixed on less exciting subjects, and in consequence gained more attention. The Chartist Riots of 1839 were the occasion of his first successful effort, and of his really gaining the ear of the House. It was remarkable, too, as showing that he was not in the ordinary sense of the word a Party man—that the Conservatives could claim him just as little as either the Radicals or the Whigs, that he had thought out the principles of the British Constitution for himself, and had come to certain practical conclusions which have been the guide of his political life. He condemned, as all men did, the scenes of violence and riot of which the Chartists had been guilty; but he insisted that it was unwise to refuse to listen to their complaints; that their very violence showed they had grievances to complain of, and those of a substantial kind; and he pointed out the mistake that had been committed in the first Reform Bill by suppressing the burgess freemen, who were in truth the representatives of the working classes, without giving those classes any share of the representation in another way. A Government founded on a middle class, said Mr. Disraeli, cannot last. In fact, a careful study of that speech will afford a key to the whole of Mr. Disraeli's career, whether in or out of office.

We need not follow the progress of the quarrel with Sir Robert Peel, which went on with increasing bitterness till Sir Robert Peel was driven from power. It is enough to say that Mr. Disraeli's speeches on those occasions, reprehensible as they might be on some grounds, stamped him as one of the first Parliamentary orators of the day. His prediction was now realised—the day had indeed come when the House would listen to him. He came down from his old seat on one of the back benches, and took up his position on the front seat below the gangway, from which some of his finest orations were delivered; and this fact gives a point to the story sometimes told of him that when a Conservative deputation invited him to resign the leadership he routed them at once by saying that in that event he should certainly take up a position on the front seat below the gangway. Peel himself now recognised in him a foeman worthy of his steel, and replied to his attacks in some of his happiest oratorical efforts, while the underlings on both sides of the House went about insinuating all sorts of base motives for his conduct. It was said that he had applied to Peel, on the formation of his Government, for an office of great responsibility, which was refused in a curt style, and that this was the secret of his subsequent opposition to the Minister. Mr. Disraeli, characteristically enough, was the first to notice this insinuation, and crushed it effectually. It was true, he said, that he had applied to the Minister for office. But he did not think any one could accuse him of arrogance in asking for the particular office he applied for. It was only for a foreign consulship, and he ventured to think the House would not consider that that was a post for which he was incompetent or disqualified. But after the refusal he had continued to support the Minister as steadily as before. He did not desert the Minister till the Minister had deserted his principles.

The sensation created by the publication of *Coningsby* and *Sybil*, in 1844 and 1845, regarded merely as social satires, will not readily be forgotten. But the political ideas which they contained, though bitterly ridiculed by a generation incapable of understanding them, became in time the foundation of a new faith. Nor can there be the slightest doubt that the great Tory Party which Mr. Disraeli led to victory in 1874 was largely indebted for its success to the principles which he had promulgated exactly thirty years before. It is perfectly true that the Toryism which was presented to the world through the medium of these brilliant fictions was an ideal Toryism, and could hardly have been reproduced in modern England any more than Plato's

Republic could have been reproduced in ancient Greece. It was founded partly on a study of Lord Bolingbroke, without due allowance being made for the difference between Parliamentary Government in the reign of Queen Victoria and Parliamentary Government in the reign of George II. Bolingbroke saw only the abuses which flourished under the system of Walpole. He could not foresee the glories of Chatham and his famous son. He very naturally attributed the first to the system introduced at the Revolution, and he as naturally turned for a remedy to the system which presented the greatest contrast to it—the Monarchy, namely, of the Tudors and Plantagenets. In the middle of the eighteenth century the revival of such a Monarchy had not become absolutely impossible. But thirty years ago it had, and the weak point in *Coningsby* and *Sybil* was that they vaguely suggested the restoration of such a polity as the remedy for prevailing evils.

But that the more important part of the theory— the doctrine, namely, that Toryism and not Radicalism ought to be the popular political creed of this country —was capable of being adapted to modern politics Mr. Disraeli has himself shown. And he performed an inestimable service to his own party by recalling to the public mind what Toryism really had been within the memory of living men, who had sat in the House of Commons before the French Revolution, and who remembered it as the party of progress. He showed that in genuine Toryism there was nothing inconsistent with political liberality. But the movement which from the publication of these works was identified with the name of Mr. Disraeli was a social as well as a political movement. Who does not remember Young England, with its white waistcoats, and its village maypoles, and its dainty feudalism? And yet, as a living writer has pointed out, what was said of another great movement of the day was equally applicable to this. Its sentiment was true. With much that was extravagant on the surface, the fundamental ideas of the Young England creed touched the heart of the rising generation. "Men began to feel that the relations between Sovereign and subject, between landlord and tenant, between gentle and simple, between priest and parishioner, might be 'beautified and sweetened.' As far as the movement aimed at a revival merely of ancient customs it was harmless and ineffective, and in some measure was laughed down. But the spirit which those customs had once represented was awakened from a long sleep, and it is impossible to deny that the relations between the different orders of society have benefited by the revival."

The Corn Law struggle, and the part which Mr. Disraeli took in it, form a portion of the general history of the country. It may be granted that he and the party with whom he acted, and who had elected Lord George Bentinck as their head, were mistaken in their opinion as to the general effect of the Free-trade policy upon the fortunes of the country. There is this to be said for them, that they were following the traditional policy of both Whigs and Tories, and that their opposition was based at least as much on the injury they believed the repeal of the laws would inflict on the working classes as on the blow it would give to their own order. Much also must be allowed to the natural feeling of high-minded Englishmen, who felt that they had been betrayed, and found the Minister whom they had borne on their shoulders into office for the purpose of maintaining Protection the first to strike it down. They were resolved that such treachery should not go unpunished, and for this purpose their leaders had recourse to a policy which probably in cooler moments they would hardly have approved, but which in the heat and irritation of those times appeared to be more than justified. On this point the reader may consult some remarks made by King Leopold, to be found in the recently published *Life of the Prince Consort*. In the same Session in which Sir Robert Peel had introduced his Bill for the repeal of the Corn Laws in the Commons, he introduced a Coercion Bill for Ireland in the Lords. This latter passed rapidly through the Upper House. But in the House of Commons the whole Protectionist Party ranged themselves against the

Minister. The Bill was rejected. Sir Robert Peel resigned, and the Whigs returned to office.

At this time the men upon whom the leader of the Opposition could actually depend for a division were fewer than one hundred and fifty, and when Lord George Bentinck divided the House upon his Motion concerning Irish railways, supposed to be his strongest point, he mustered to his colours but one hundred and eighteen members. It seemed as if the "great Conservative Party" was about to disappear altogether, and the task which devolved on Mr. Disraeli in 1848 was much harder than the task which devolved on Sir Robert Peel in 1833, inasmuch as the feeble remnant which supported him was unsustained by the consciousness of any great principle for the sake of which it had so suddenly been brought low.

The first thing to be done was, in Mr. Disraeli's estimation, the recovery of the rank and file of the Peelites to the Conservative cause. For this purpose he devised a series of motions which should have the effect of accustoming them to find themselves in the same lobby with their former associates, and the success of his tactics soon became apparent in the increasing numbers which year after year he was able to muster against Government. In 1849 his best division was 189 against 280. In 1850 he had detached twenty-two members from the Ministerial side, and was beaten by a majority of only twenty-one, Mr. Gladstone himself, for the first time since 1846, being seen in opposition to Sir Robert Peel. In 1851 Mr. Disraeli divided 267 against 281, a result which contributed in no small degree to the resignation of Ministers soon afterwards. Lord Stanley, however, after vainly appealing to Mr. Gladstone, to whom Mr. Disraeli would at that time have surrendered the lead of the House of Commons, declined the formation of a Government, and Lord Russell was obliged to resume office. But in the following year he was again driven to resign, and this time the leader of the party—who had now become Lord Derby—felt himself compelled to form a Ministry. It is not to be wondered that he shrank from doing so. With a Cabinet of recruits he had to face a majority of veterans.

The new Ministry, in which Mr. Disraeli filled the office of Chancellor of the Exchequer, began in a minority, and it was understood that no opposition would be offered to a winding up of the work of the Session then pending, and that after this there should be an appeal to the country. There was, therefore, a comparative truce from Party struggles within the walls of Parliament. But a very different scene was enacted out of doors. A period of six years had now elapsed since the abolition of the Corn Laws; and though some extreme members of the Tory Party still muttered their discontent and their resolution to endeavour to effect a change, the great body of them had long before withdrawn from the strife, and tacitly acquiesced in the inevitable.

But the Liberals were not slow to discern how effective as a Party war-cry would be the imputation of a Protectionist policy. The machinery of the Anti-Corn Law League was hastily resuscitated, meetings were held in the manufacturing towns, at which the leading Freetraders put down their names for fabulous sums of money, in the event, which they had good reason to know would not occur, of the Government attempting to reverse the policy of the previous six years; and by these and similar means the country was stimulated to return a majority adverse to the Government. The decisive issue was taken on the Budget. It was the first effort of Mr. Disraeli as a Finance Minister, and considerable curiosity was felt as to the result. He did not disappoint the public expectation. In a speech which lasted five hours he took a masterly review of the financial position of the country. He proposed to render taxation more equal in its pressure; and, starting from the assumption that taxation and representation should go together, he proposed that the house duty should be carried down as low as the franchise, and laid upon houses of 10*l.* value. He proposed a reduction of the malt duties, while, as a counterpoise, he suggested that they should deal in the same liberal spirit with the duties on tea. Such were the salient features of the Budget. In consequence, however, of the tactics of the Opposition, the financial statement of the Government was made in December, 1852, instead of in March, 1853, as would have been the usual course. By the latter date Mr. Disraeli was in the habit of asserting that the disappearance of agricultural distress would have enabled him to frame a Budget untainted by the slightest odour of Protectionist opinions. At the earlier date this was impossible; the Opposition knew this as well as he did, and forced his hand accordingly. A coalition took place between the Whigs, the Peelites, and the Radicals, and the result was that Government were beaten by a majority of nineteen. The Tory Party, however, were upon the whole very well satisfied. They had played a losing game with spirit. They had held office with credit. They felt that their leaders had been tried and not found wanting; and they waited with confidence in their tact and statesmanship till a fresh opportunity should occur.

That opportunity occurred and was lost in 1855, on the resignation of Lord Aberdeen, when Lord Derby, much to the chagrin of Mr. Disraeli, declined to take office without the assistance of Lord Palmerston and Mr. Gladstone. It was Lord Derby's own Parliament, and another dissolution would probably have given him a majority. However, he declined the responsibility, and the ball rolled to the feet of Lord Palmerston, who seized the opportunity, for which perhaps he had long been waiting, and at the mature age of seventy-one became Prime Minister of England. During the Crimean war the Conservative Party gave a loyal support to the Government. And during the negotiations which followed Mr. Disraeli first began to show that intimate acquaintance with foreign affairs which made many people suppose that he was marked out for Foreign Minister. In 1858 a mistake of Lord Palmerston's brought the Tories into office once more; and as men had been curious to see how in 1852 they would deal with Protection, so were they curious now to see how they would deal with Parliamentary Reform. Lord John Russell had revived the question in 1852; and it had been fitfully discussed ever since. Mr. Disraeli, as leader of the Conservatives, was called upon to take part in these debates, and he showed in his speeches that he was not disposed to offer a blind and dogged resistance to the cry, but would rather, if that were possible, guide the movement which could not be repressed. He dilated on the defects of the first Reform Bill, on the injustice done to the counties in the distribution of seats, and on the wrong done to the working classes by the extinction of the scot and lot voters. At the same time he insisted that reform, to be beneficial, ought to be extended in a lateral rather than in a downward direction, and that any measure of enfranchisement ought to include all the intelligence and education of the country, and reach those classes of the community that were not to be found in the occupation of £10 houses. A Reform Bill in conformity with Mr. Disraeli's views was eventually determined on by the Government. Ministers, however, had a narrow escape of shipwreck before they had a chance of unfolding it. A vote of censure was prepared by the Opposition in connection with a despatch sent out by Lord Ellenborough to India. It was debated four nights in the House of Commons, but by degrees the truth oozed out that the despatch had been completely justified, and the sudden breaking up of the Opposition phalanx was graphically described by Mr. Disraeli in a speech at Slough, which was long remembered as one of his most brilliant efforts.

The following year the first Derby Reform Bill was brought in. The county and borough franchise were fixed at the same level of £10, and in the redistribution of seats a larger number than before was given to the counties. Though the borough franchise was not reduced, yet the number of the electors was to be largely added to by votes being given to those who possessed a certain sum in the savings banks, or who gave other guarantees of intelligence and social position. Only one of Mr. Disraeli's ideas was not carried out—that which proposed to remedy the injustice of the first Reform Bill by conferring the suffrage on the working classes. The time for that step was not yet come. The Ministerial measure, however, was rejected. Lord Derby resigned, and the Saturnian age of Lord Palmerston began.

Session rolled by after Session with little more than the yearly routine of measures, and agitation was everywhere so much discouraged that Mr. Bright declared that he despaired of any further reform during Lord Palmerston's lifetime. The Paper Duties and the Commercial Treaty with France agitated both Houses. But Foreign Affairs were the dominant subject of interest—the cession of Savoy and Nice, the affairs of Poland and Denmark, and the civil war raging in America. On all and each of these Mr. Disraeli spoke with great ability, especially on the Danish question, which drew from him, on the 4th of July, 1864, one of the most masterly *résumés* of our then recent foreign policy to be found in Parliamentary annals. As the Parliament of 1859 approached its seventh Session it became evident that Lord Palmerston had taken the measure of his countrymen more accurately than his reforming colleagues imagined, for at the general election of 1865 a large majority was returned to the House of Commons whose main political character was that they were pledged to support Lord Palmerston.

Thus the prospect of a speedy return of the Conservatives to power appeared more hopeless than ever.

But great changes were at hand. Lord Palmerston died in the autumn of that year, and the duty of meeting the new Parliament fell to Earl Russell as Premier, with Mr. Gladstone as leader in the House of Commons. Then the long-repressed energies of these statesmen broke out; and it was announced that the first measure of the reconstructed Ministry would be a new Reform Bill, with a £6 suffrage. The precipitation with which this measure was adopted annoyed many of the friends of Lord Palmerston. The Reform Bill was opposed by the Conservatives, Mr. Disraeli taking up his old line, that this monotonous franchise put the government of the country into the hands of one class of the community, and allowed no free play to the great variety of classes and interests of which the community is made up. The opposition to the Bill, however, at least in Committee, was for the most part initiated by discontented Liberals, whose Cave of Adullam has become an historic bye-word. It soon became evident that Ministers did not possess force enough to force the measure through. Still, Mr. Gladstone persevered, until an amendment by a Whig member that the franchise should be based on the rating, and not the mere rental-value, placed the Ministers in a minority, and the Russell-Gladstone Government was at an end.

The private history of the Reform Bill of 1867 has still to be written; but we may be permitted to say here that all the gossip that was current at that time, and has been current since, concerning what Mr. Lowe called "the unparalleled betrayal" of the Tory party by its leader, was due either to an ignorance of the facts of the case, which one can scarcely conceive probable, or to an intentional perversion of the truth, which we should be sorry to think possible. The Reform Bill of 1867—good, bad, or indifferent—was essentially the work of the House of Commons. The Cabinet decided—in fact, they had no alternative—to introduce a measure of reform. It was evident that somebody must do it; it was equally evident that Ministers with majorities had failed to do it; and Mr. Disraeli, therefore, wisely determined, if he could, to remove the question from the domain of Party, and to make the whole House of Commons co-operate with him in his work. This was the meaning of his celebrated thirteen "Resolutions," by which he hoped to ascertain the collective opinion of the House, so as to frame a measure which could not be assailed on purely Party grounds. As the success of this proposal would have had the effect of disarming the Opposition, its leaders, of course, rejected it, and the Cabinet was compelled to bring in a Bill at once. But none the less was Mr. Disraeli's idea successful in the end, and the whole House itself made to co-operate in a measure which neither Party by itself appeared by itself capable of passing.

The scheme which subsequently received the Royal assent, and which had been the original design of Lord Derby and Mr. Disraeli, was abandoned, in the first instance, in deference to the feelings of other members of the Cabinet. But few people know what it cost Mr. Disraeli to propose the measure which had been kept in reserve as a substitute, instead of the bolder one which he had matured himself. Very short notice was given to him of the inability of Lord Salisbury, Lord Carnarvon, and General Peel to support the latter. Mr. Disraeli had hardly more than one day to prepare himself for the task; and it may not be generally known that he offered to resign office rather than break up the Cabinet or undertake a task so much to his own distaste.

However, he was overruled. But at three o'clock in the afternoon of that day he had eaten nothing, and, after taking a single glass of wine in Downing Street, he went down to the House, there to discharge his allotted task, with an air of depression and depreciation which surprised every one who heard him. The Bill, however, was only born to perish, and the Ministry and the Conservative Party had now to consider what course they were to take The decision was not left to the Government. A meeting was held at the Carlton Club, the result of which was to inform the Prime Minister and the Chancellor of the Exchequer that the Tory Party now would support the original scheme, and no other. Thus, so far from Mr. Disraeli having dragged an unwilling Party after him, the Party itself insisted on his acting as he did, and he had no sincerer supporters through the desperate struggles which ensued than some of those very county members whose trust he was said to have abused.

Whatever may be thought of the policy of the Government measure, there is no doubt that Mr. Disraeli's Parliamentary reputation was enormously enhanced by his conduct of it. So bitter and ruthless an opposition has rarely been met by such consummate tact, such immovable good temper, such alert logic, and such perfect self-possession. His humorous comments on Mr. Gladstone's fierce attacks delighted both sides of the House, and his stinging repartees on gentlemen who assailed him in flank will long be remembered. The easy good humour with which he expressed his satisfaction at having the table between himself and Mr. Gladstone during one of that gentleman's most indignant diatribes destroyed its whole effect in a moment.

Nor were his graver efforts less surprising. One night he wound up a great debate, answering the House all round in a speech of three hours' duration, without a single note, and it was generally allowed that he had not missed a point, or failed to make the most of an argument. When, after his first great division against the whole might of Mr.

Gladstone, which he won by a majority of twenty-one, Tory members crowded up to the Treasury bench to shake hands with and congratulate him, they only expressed the feeling of the rest of the House, who would have liked to pay the same tribute of admiration to so genial and gallant an antagonist. *A propos* of this triumph, Lady Beaconsfield delighted to tell how, after it was over, an ovation was prepared for him at the Carlton, where the younger members of the Party begged him to remain to supper; and how, in spite of their seductions, he came home to his wife and ate half the raised pie, and finished the bottle of champagne, which she had prepared for his reception.

The most notable event in the career of Mr. Disraeli during the remainder of the year 1867 was the famous Edinburgh banquet, when he took credit to himself for having "educated" the Tories and taught them to recur to the principles of its founders, and to be the popular Party. But what that famous speech will long be remembered for was the inimitable comparison of the *Edinburgh* and *Quarterly Reviews* to the two old-fashioned rival posting-houses. They had both attacked his policy as dangerous, revolutionary, and precipitate. So, said he, may you behold the ostler at the Blue Lion and the chambermaid at the King's Arms, though bitter rivals in the bygone epoch of coaches and post-horses, making up their quarrels and condoling together in the street over their common enemy the railroad.

In the Session of 1868 Mr. Disraeli was chiefly occupied with the completion of his Reform Bill, by extending its provisions to Scotland, and with a measure for the prevention of bribery and corruption. But the real interest of the Session began with the resignation of Lord Derby, on the 25th of February. Mr. Disraeli might have said, with Canning, that the post was his by inheritance, and the enthusiastic cheers which greeted him as he walked up to his seat the first night of his appearance as Premier, sufficiently showed that his claim to the dignity was recognised. The celebrated Irish Church Resolutions were the immediate result of Mr. Disraeli's assumption of the Premiership, and though Mr. Disraeli spoke against them with great power, it was manifest that the conclusion was foregone. Resistance was hopeless in that Parliament. But Mr. Disraeli no doubt expected better things from a new one. The result of the elections, however, was so decisive that he at once resigned, and Mr. Gladstone had time to prepare his measures for the next Session.

During the earlier Sessions of Mr. Gladstone's first Administration little was left to the Opposition but to record an unavailing protest against the revolutionary measures which it succeeded in carrying. Mr. Disraeli had little to add in 1869 to what he said in 1868, though he had the additional mortification of knowing that it must be said in vain. The battle of the Irish Church was really fought at the General Election. But such was not the case with the Irish Land Bill, though even on this subject it was too early to expect that the overwhelming Liberal majority would listen to the voice of reason. But in the following year, when Mr. Gladstone's Irish policy was well out of the way—when the storm of excitement which had first borne him into office had begun to subside, and at last there seemed some chance of opposing Ministers with effect—Mr. Disraeli " woke up again," as was said at the time, and very early in the Session of 1871 delivered a most vigorous and witty speech upon the Government proposal for a select Parliamentary Committee to inquire into the condition of Westmeath.

It was in this speech that he summed up the policy of Ministers in the following memorable sentences:—" The right hon. gentleman persuaded the people of England that with regard to Irish politics he was in possession of the philosopher's stone. He has been returned to this House with an immense majority, with the object of securing the tranquillity and content of Ireland. Has anything been grudged him? Time, labour, devotion— whatever has been demanded has been accorded; whatever has been proposed has been carried.

Under his influence, and at his instance, we have legalised confiscation, consecrated sacrilege, and condoned high treason; we have destroyed Churches, we have shaken property to its foundation, and we have emptied gaols; and now he cannot govern a county without coming to a Select Committee. The right hon. gentleman, after all his heroic exploits, and at the head of his great majority, is making Government ridiculous." The roars of laughter and cheering which this pungent rhetoric evoked will never be forgotten by any one who had the luck to hear them.

This was not, however, the first great speech which he made this Session. Three days before he had delivered a most cutting philippic on the proposed Black Sea Conference, more particularly with reference to the declaration of Mr. Odo Russell to Prince Bismarck, to the effect that the act of Russia in violating the neutrality of the Black Sea would be a *casus belli* for England either with or without allies. There can be little doubt that with the beginning of this Session, 1871, began the first decline of the Government in public estimation. But it was with the year 1872 that the handwriting on the wall first became visible to all whom the evil genius of Liberalism had not blinded. Ministers had lived, as Mr. Disraeli said, in a "blaze of apology" during the preceding autumn; and in the following Session two things occurred which shook the Cabinet to its centre—their adoption of the Ballot Bill, and their policy towards Mr. Fawcett's Dublin University Bill. The history of the latter transaction could not be adequately explained without the previous history of Mr. Fawcett's measure, which would be out of place on this occasion. It may be sufficient to state that Mr. Bouverie, sitting just behind Mr. Gladstone, stigmatised it as "inconsistent with the dignity of the Sovereign, disrespectful to the House of Commons, and repugnant to the feelings of gentlemen."

Mr. Disraeli was far too skilful a tactician to mar the effect of this scathing invective from one of the supporters of the Government by adding anything of his own to it. But by narrowly watching the effect which it produced in a House of Commons devoted to the Premier, he was able to draw pretty just inferences as to the state of public feeling out of doors. The Ballot debates were even more damaging to Ministers, for it was conclusively shown that they had not taken up the measure till the alleged necessity for it was confessedly passing away. The Premier, said Mr. Disraeli, had "passionately embraced a corpse," and he was heard to say on more than one occasion in private, and with great energy, that he "hated the Ballot," and we have reason to believe that his opinion of it never changed.

It was in the spring of this year—*i.e.*, Easter, 1872

—that Mr. Disraeli fulfilled a promise given the year before to the Conservatives of Lancashire, and paid a political visit to the great centres of our commercial and manufacturing industries. The invitation had been accepted in 1871, coupled with the intimation that Mr. Disraeli would prefer to choose his own time for fulfilling the engagement. And now the time had arrived. His progress was one perpetual triumph. The enthusiastic reception which he experienced from the working classes was unmarred by a single hostile manifestation. The speech which he delivered at Manchester was well worthy of the occasion, but over all that dignified eloquence shone pre-eminent the peerless wit which likened the then occupants of the Treasury Bench to "a series of extinct volcanoes." But the Ballot Act was the last of their eruptions, and with the Session of 1873 it became tolerably apparent that the end was not far off. Before the opening of the new year, however, Mr. Disraeli had suffered a domestic loss which, it was feared, would, for a long time at least, banish him from public affairs. In December, 1872, "the perfect wife," she who had really fulfilled for him all which conventional courtesy attributes to the gentler sex—who had gloried in his triumphs, lightened his reverses; and whose sympathy with his political career was the genuine product of her nature—whose devoted love shed over his home even to the last something of the bloom and softness of early married life—Maria, Lady Beaconsfield, died at an advanced age, and left the bereaved statesman to "the darkest hour of his existence." Nevertheless, it was, perhaps, because her sympathy with his public life had been so deep and genuine that Mr. Disraeli may have found his best solace in renewing it, and have felt that in pursuing such a course he was not yet entirely dissevered from her. At all events, he returned to Parliamentary work with apparently unflagging energies, and circumstances soon occurred which showed that his political nerve, his coolness, and his prescience were still perfect. Mr. Gladstone's fate had at last come upon him, and he was compelled to fight on Mr. Fawcett's Dublin University Bill. Beaten by a majority of three, he at once tendered his resignation, and without a moment's delay her Majesty sent for Mr. Disraeli. He declined to form a Government at once, he and Lord Derby having previously made up their minds what to do in the contingency which happened. Mr. Disraeli informed her Majesty that he should have no difficulty in constructing an Administration, but that he would not undertake to do so with the existing House of Commons. Eventually, after the most desperate efforts to dislodge his antagonist from the position in which he had entrenched himself, and to force him to come down and take office, Mr. Gladstone was compelled to go back again, and it was generally supposed he would dissolve Parliament at once. He gave it to be understood, however, that he felt himself under no obligation to do so, and the prevailing opinion began to be that he would tide over another Session. The event justified Mr. Disraeli's foresight; but even had it not, nobody can deny that he was right and Mr. Gladstone wrong on the question of Parliamentary conduct. To say, as Mr. Gladstone did, that when a Minister is defeated and resigns the leader of the Opposition is bound to take office in his place, is to say that no leader of Opposition who is not ready to take office ought to press his resistance so far as to defeat the Government. Now, as a leader of Opposition can, in the nature of things, only be in this condition under circumstances which occur at rare intervals, it follows from Mr. Gladstone's doctrine that for the greater part of their time Prime Ministers shall be virtually absolute, exposed only to abstract criticism, which is never to be carried to any practical result. There were members of the Tory party, we believe, who, though they did not doubt the correctness of Mr. Disraeli's theory, doubted the soundness of his judgment in not taking office and dissolving when he had the chance. And it is impossible to say even now what might have happened if Mr. Gladstone had given himself the chance of another Session, and had conjured up some other blazing question with which to dazzle public opinion. The probability is, however, that nothing of the kind could have been done in the existing House of Commons. The energies of the party were distracted and exhausted, Government was beaten and demoralised, and it is probable that Mr. Gladstone's best chance lay in doing what he did, and trying for a new House of Commons with a smaller majority, kept in order by the danger of a powerful and sanguine Opposition. Mr. Disraeli justified himself to his supporters in words of memorable import:—" I believe that the Tory Party at the present time occupies the most satisfactory position which it has held since the days of its greatest statesmen—Mr. Pitt and Lord Grenville. It has divested itself of those excrescences which are not indigenous to its native growth, but which, in a time of long prosperity, were the consequences partly of negligence, and partly, perhaps, in a certain degree of its traditions. We are now emerging from the fiscal period. . . . . But there are other questions . . . . which must soon engage the country. The attributes of a Constitutional Monarchy—whether the aristocratic principle should be recognised in our Constitution— whether the Commons of England shall continue an estate of the realm, or degenerate into an indiscriminate multitude—whether a National Church shall be maintained—the functions of corporations, the sanctity of endowments, the tenure of landed property— all those institutions and principles which have made this country free and famous, and conspicuous for its union of order with liberty, are now impugned, and, in due time, will become great and 'burning' questions. I think it is of the utmost importance that when that time arrives which may be nearer at hand than we imagine, there shall be in this country a great Constitutional Party which shall be competent to lead the people and direct the public mind. And, sir, when that time arrives, and they enter on a career which must be noble, and which I hope and believe will be triumphant, I think they may perhaps remember—and not perhaps with unkindness—that I at least prevented one obstacle from being thrown in their way, when, as the trustee of their honour and their interests, I declined to form a weak and discredited Administration." In the following autumn he was installed Lord Rector of the University of Glasgow, an honour which was repeated in 1874, when he defeated Mr. Emerson, by a majority of 200. Two months afterwards the world was taken by surprise by the announcement of a dissolution of Parliament.

The result of the General Election placed Mr. Disraeli in office, with a clear majority of fifty; and we may now view him as having realised for a time the dream of his youth, and the more practical conceptions of his riper years, in the establishment of the claim of the Tory Party to be the "popular political confederation of this country." Some people attributed the Tory victory to the wrath of the licensed victuallers, some to a religious panic, some to both, and "beer and the Bible" was a favourite taunt which the defeated Liberals hurled at the heads of their antagonists. But though no doubt these exasperated "interests" did swell the Tory majority, a deeper and more permanent feeling than anything which these ephemeral wrongs could have produced was the mainspring of the movement. The people had begun to recognise in the Tory Party the existence of qualities which, however obscured during their more recent history, had never been totally extinguished, and had once been their distinctive badge. They felt, in a word, that under all the objectionable policy attributed to Toryism, supposing the imputation to be true, there lay a fund of national sentiment and a loyalty to English ideas not equally discernible in their rivals. Great revulsions of popular feeling are seldom attributable to specific grievances. These may fire the train, but more general causes must have laid it. And that some such general notions as we have here described were largely diffused among the working classes at the General Election of 1874 we think there can be no doubt. Nor is the result of the last General Election really inconsistent with this conclusion.

It may be remembered that Mr. Disraeli's Government came into office to some extent pledged to the redress of grievances under which various

D

important interests conceived themselves to be suffering. The army believed itself wronged by Mr. Cardwell's Army Bill. The licensed victuallers had been injured by Mr. Bruce's Licensing Act. The Church had been unjustly treated by Mr. Forster's Education Act, and it was an understood thing that whenever the Tory Party returned to power an effort should be made to do justice to these various complaints. But independently of the work which the policy of the late Government had directly prepared for its successor, there were other grievances not indeed created by that Administration, but with which it had wholly failed to cope, and to the redress of which the Opposition had more or less committed itself. First and foremost among these stood the grievance of the local ratepayers, represented in the House of Commons by a band of able men of business, and flushed with their victory over Mr. Gladstone in 1872, when Sir Massey Lopes defeated the Government by a majority of one hundred. Next in importance stood the operative class, who felt themselves aggrieved by the Labour Laws, the existing Factory Acts, and the progressive inclosure of waste lands and commons. Last, but not least, came tenant farmers, who were anxious for some readjustment of our system of land tenure, and also looked forward to some more effective measure than had yet been passed for the exclusion of cattle disease from these islands.

Besides these various questions there were others of more general interest which demanded investigation; such as the state of our prisons, the condition of our mercantile marine, the whole system of our county administration, the Burial Laws, and, as a matter of course, the Bankruptcy Laws. Here, then, were subjects enough to occupy the attention of any Government without rekindling those volcanic fires which had so long shed their lurid glare over the Liberal Administration. Mr. Disraeli accordingly found himself entering upon office with a powerful and united majority, to carry out that very programme which twenty-two years before had been sketched out by the late Lord Derby as the one he intended to pursue. Now, at last, Mr. Disraeli had an opportunity of proving whether his sympathy with the working classes had been merely assumed for party purposes or whether it was sincere and lasting. The world was not long left in doubt. One of the first measures introduced into the House of Commons by the new Home Secretary, Mr. Cross, was a Factory Bill for the protection of women; and one of the next an Employers and Workmen Bill for the rectification of legal inequalities complained of by the workmen. From that time to the end of the Parliament the same course of legislation was steadily pursued, not a Session passing without some contribution being made to the Statute Book in the interests of the working man, designed either to consult his self-respect, to ensure his safety, or to promote his comfort and convenience. We need only name the Artisans' Dwellings Bill, the Enclosure of Commons Bill, the Friendly Societies Bill, the Public Health Bill, and, finally, the Factory Act Consolidation Bill of 1878.

The more specific pledges given by the Conservatives in Opposition Mr. Disraeli took care to redeem as soon as he came into power. A Licensing Amendment Act relieved the keepers of public-houses from the more oppressive and vexatious regulations of Mr. Bruce's measure. An Education Amendment Act enabled denominational schools to compete on something like an equal footing with the Board schools. The Regimental Exchanges Bill satisfied the officers of the army. The Agricultural Holdings Act was welcomed by the farmers' friends in the House of Commons as changing the presumption of law in favour of the farmer, though that such a change has not had much practical effect is shown by the vigorous efforts now being made by Mr. Chaplin and other Conservative county members to make the Act really operative instead of being, as it is, merely permissive. Finally the local rates received substantial instalments of relief by the Rating Act of 1874, the Poor-law Amendment Act of 1876, the Prisons Act of 1877, and the Highways Act of 1878. Neither the Prisons Bill nor the Cattle Bill, however, was intended especially for the benefit of any one class in the community. They were national and popular measures, of which the primary objects were to deal more effectively with criminals, and to protect the flocks and herds of the country from being decimated by imported disease.

Thus it will be seen that down to 1878 Mr. Disraeli's Government had really done all or nearly all which it had undertaken to do on coming into power, besides passing many other measures of the first degree of public importance. The work of the Cabinet was performed gradually; and as it did not deal with "burning" questions, never filled that space in the public eye which was filled by Mr. Gladstone's legislation. But for real solid utility, and the benefits which it has conferred on all classes of society, it will contrast very favourably with the work of the preceding Government—with amending which, indeed, a good deal of the time of the Tory party was taken up.

There were other questions, no doubt, in which his Government was less fortunate. The Church of England was gratified by Lord Sandon's Education Act, by the Endowed Schools Act Amendment Act, and by the Bishoprics Acts. But, unhappily, the Public Worship Regulation Act did not for a long time effect the object of its authors; and Government found itself unable to settle the Burial question, in spite of the compromise which was offered to the Dissenters. But it must be borne in mind that neither of these failures can be laid to the door of Lord Beaconsfield or any of the members of his Cabinet. The Public Worship Regulation Act was the work of the Bench of Bishops, who were deeply convinced of its necessity. The Bishop of Gloucester declared that if the Bill had not been passed the Establishment would not have lasted five years. The rest of the Bishops, with a single exception, were unanimous, and Mr. Disraeli, though personally not in favour of the measure, felt that he could not well oppose himself to this weight of authority. When we say that he was personally not in favour of it, we mean that he was probably prescient of its consequences. But he never viewed with approbation the attempts of the ultra-High Churchmen to revive in the English Church a system which, if not illegal, was at least obsolete, and opposed, as he believed, to the deep-seated feeling of the vast majority of the people.

Whether he was right or wrong in this estimate of the subject is another question; whether nothing which is obsolete can ever be revived with advantage, or whether so large a majority of the English people are really hostile to Ritualism, cannot be positively decided. And it is true that among Mr. Disraeli's strong points, a knowledge of the English Church, with a just appreciation of its parties, its traditions, and its susceptibilities, was not to be reckoned. Still, on this matter of Ritual he would have left the Clergy alone, if the Bishops would have left his Government alone. But they would not, and between them the Public Worship Regulation Act became law—a measure so certain to provoke misconstruction, and, therefore, to encourage disobedience, that it might have been wiser, perhaps, in the Minister of the day to abstain from supporting it.

With regard to the Burial question, however, Mr. Disraeli's Government, though even more unfortunate, was even more completely blameless. To what extent the Bishops, and more especially the Primate, had been consulted before the Burials Bill of 1876 was introduced into the House of Lords we are not, of course, aware; but it received their cordial support as soon as it was introduced. But directly an Amendment was proposed which went straight to the principle of the Bill and destroyed the essence of the compromise, the Archbishop of Canterbury turned round and gave that Amendment his support. Of course, after this the fate of the Bill was sealed. Two other questions besides were left over to the present Government which the former one would have been wise to settle—the Game Question and County Administration; and the failure to deal with either must be allowed to be a blot on Mr. Disraeli's domestic legislation.

We must now, however, turn to the time when it was announced that the days of Lord Beaconsfield in the House of Commons were numbered, and that failing health warned him from a scene in which he had so long drunk delight of battle with his peers, and in which he had never seemed so great as when striving against tremendous odds. Mr. Disraeli made his last speech in the House of Commons on the 11th of August, 1876. Next morning the well-kept secret was disclosed. Mr. Disraeli was to become Earl of Beaconsfield, and the leadership of the House of Commons was to devolve upon Sir Stafford Northcote. Physical incapacity to bear any longer the fatigue of leading the House of Commons was his only motive for the step. And it must have been with no common emotion that he took his leave of an arena in which he had experienced such remarkable vicissitudes of good and ill fortune, and had crowned a chequered career with a brilliant and popular triumph.

It cannot be said that in the accomplished and courteous lieutenant whom he left behind him in the House of Commons, Lord Beaconsfield had provided it with a leader equal to himself, able either to rein that proud Assembly with the same firm hand, or to wield the magic blade which its master in so many gallant fights had indeed borne "like a king." The last person in the world to claim any such equality would be Sir Stafford Northcote himself. But still in ordinary times it is probable that he would have been found quite equal to the duties of his position, and that Lord Beaconsfield's absence from his old post would have caused little or no remark. But his lot, unfortunately, was not cast in ordinary times. Sir Stafford Northcote was new to his difficult position in times of extraordinary difficulty, confronted by novel phenomena in the House of Commons itself, and by a crisis of stupendous gravity in the foreign relations of this country. That the long Parliamentary experience, the strength of character, the fertility of resource, the eloquence, the wit, and the satire which gave Mr. Disraeli an ascendency in the House of Commons equal to that of either Sir Robert Peel or Lord Palmerston, would have made comparatively short work of the Irish Obstructives, and would have bestowed on the attacks of the Opposition the chastisement which they deserved, may be asserted with confidence, and without any unjust depreciation of Sir Stafford Northcote. Had he remained in the Lower House, it is probable, indeed, that the Home Rulers would never have carried their tactics to the length they did; and that we should have been spared the disgraceful scenes of 1877 and 1878. But if the representation of Foreign Affairs in the House of Commons during those two Sessions had devolved on Mr. Disraeli, it is far from impossible that the effort might have cost him his life.

It was early in 1876 that the Eastern Question began to attract the notice of the general public in this country. We may pass over its earlier incidents, the Andrassy Note and the Berlin Memorandum, and come at once to the more exciting events which threatened at one time the very existence of Lord Beaconsfield's Ministry. It was in March, 1876, that rumours began to reach this country of atrocious outrages perpetrated by the Bashi-Bazouks in suppressing the Bulgarian insurrection. At first they were discredited by the Government. But the publication of Mr. Baring's report, and the appearance of some remarkable letters in the columns of a contemporary, speedily inflamed the passions of the people to fever height, and in an evil hour tempted certain eminent men to fan the flames of agitation. Reports were studiously circulated that Mr. Disraeli was indifferent to these horrors; that his "Semitic instincts" led him to sympathise with Turkey through all extremes; and that in aping the policy of Lord Palmerston he was clinging to an exploded superstition.

Lord Beaconsfield was not more indifferent to human suffering than other people, but his sagacity taught him to distrust the accuracy of these reports, and the event proved that he was right. As for aping the policy of Lord Palmerston, it became abundantly clear afterwards that if he had only aped it a little sooner, much bloodshed would have been spared, and many serious errors avoided. And as to his "Semitic instincts," the wiseacres who circulated this phrase were evidently unaware that the Semitic instincts of Lord Beaconsfield, if he had been guided only by them, taught him to hate the barbarian Turk as the ruthless oppressor of the genuine Arab race, from which he himself sprang, and which had a literature and a philosophy which the semi-savage Ottomans could not comprehend. Any reader of *Tancred* may see what Lord Beaconsfield really thought about the Turks. But when placed in a great political position, responsible for the safety of an Empire and for the happiness or misery of so many millions of the human race, his own individual opinions were obliged to give way to higher and more general considerations. He saw no way of securing a barrier against the advance of Russia to the Mediterranean on the one hand and the banks of the Euphrates on the other but by maintaining the Ottoman Empire in its place. It was on the 26th of June that he made his first important speech upon the subject, in which he dwelt on the improbability of the Turkish troops having kept any prisoners for torture, as they usually proceeded by more expeditious methods. This expression was denounced as "levity" by sour and austere fanatics. But Mr. Disraeli lived it down, as he did many other imputations, and that in a very short space of time. On the 4th of August, 1876, he made his second great speech in Parliament on this subject, when he exposed with great effect the exaggerations which had been palmed off upon the British public as trustworthy evidence of the ineradicable ferocity and brutality of the Turkish race. He likewise spoke with great dignity of what he conceived to be the duty of her Majesty's Government at this momentous crisis. Our duty, said he, is "to maintain the Empire of England," and these words gave the key-note to his policy, from which, through evil report and good report, he never afterwards deviated. All through the autumn, however, Mr. Gladstone and his disciples kept up a vigorous agitation against his policy. The state of the public mind was such during the autumn months that a general election would almost certainly have returned a Parliament pledged to a crusade against Turkey. Lord Beaconsfield took one or two opportunities of setting the public right on these matters, once at the agricultural dinner at Aylesbury in September, and again at the Lord Mayor's dinner at the Guildhall, when he observed that if England embarked in war she was not a country who would have to consider "if she could enter on a second or third campaign."

This language of course encouraged Lord Beaconsfield's enemies to declare loudly that he was bent on plunging England into war. But on the whole Lord Beaconsfield seemed himself to prefer the policy of giving his opponents rope enough, and he had no reason to reproach himself with want of foresight. As the autumn went on, public opinion began to turn. Influential Liberals like Lord Fitzwilliam and the Duke of Somerset began to denounce the violence of the Radical leaders of the Opposition. The publication of Mr. Schuyler's book informed the British public that Russia, too, could be guilty of atrocities not one shade less execrable than those imputed to the Turks; and when it was announced that Lord Salisbury was to be the English Plenipotentiary at a Conference of the Great Powers, to be held at Constantinople in December, confidence in Lord Beaconsfield's Government had been pretty well restored. Men became ashamed of their almost wilful blindness to the true character of Lord Derby's Despatch of the 21st of September. The Conference, however, was a failure. Turkey turned a deaf ear to the suggestions of reforms pressed upon her by all the European Powers, England included; and the Porte was, therefore, left to its fate. *Major martis jam apparet imago.* But still opinion was greatly divided in England on the probability of war breaking out. The meeting of Parliament, however, had enabled Ministers to make such explanations of their policy as satisfied the majority of the people, and completed the reaction which had commenced in the November previous.

Henceforth Lord Beaconsfield retained the confidence and admiration of the country to the end of the Eastern negotiations, and his opponents had the satisfaction of seeing that he had emerged from the short eclipse of his popularity more powerful and more trusted than ever. War ultimately broke out between Turkey and Russia on the 30th of April, 1877, with the progress of which it is unnecessary to detain our readers. It is sufficient to say that the gallantry exhibited by the Turkish troops won the sympathy and admiration of England; and that throughout the remainder of the Session, as well as during the recess, Lord Beaconsfield's Ministry suffered no diminution of credit. Lord Derby's Despatch to the Russian Government, and the answer returned to it, in which an assurance was given that the points specified by Lord Derby, namely, Constantinople, Egypt, and the Suez Canal, should be respected, satisfied the public mind.

When Parliament was prorogued Lord Beaconsfield's position was still as powerful as ever. The Opposition had endeavoured to foment a popular outcry against the assumption by her Majesty of the title of Empress of India, but the people, on the whole, were rather pleased with it than otherwise, and faction was once more disappointed. During the autumn of 1877 it however began to be apparent that some little divisions of opinion were creeping into the Cabinet. Lord Carnarvon and Lord Derby made speeches very different in tone from those of Mr. Hardy and Lord John Manners. But Lord Beaconsfield said very little till the Lord Mayor's dinner, when, after dwelling on the fact that Turkey had proved that she was something more than a geographical expression, he wound up by advising the public to "try a little patience." At the close of this year Lord Beaconsfield enjoyed the distinguished honour of a visit from her Majesty at Hughenden, a graceful tribute to the services of the veteran Statesman which was fully appreciated by the public.

The announcement that the Session of 1878 was to commence a month earlier than usual, and that Parliament was to meet on the 19th of January, gave rise to many agitating rumours; and when it was known that in consequence of the English Fleet having been ordered to the Dardanelles, Lord Carnarvon and Lord Derby had resigned, the party passions of an earlier period seemed to be rekindled. Lord Derby, however, resumed his place in the Government in a few days, only, however, to retain it for a short time, his final retirement being caused by a difference with his colleagues as to the proposed Congress, and according to his own account, about some project for seizing a Turkish port in Asia Minor. It was at this time that the reserve forces were called out, also a step of which Lord Derby had disapproved.

The excitement, however, created by this act of

vigour was as nothing compared with the denunciations which were launched at the head of Lord Beaconsfield when it was known that a portion of our Indian army had been ordered to Malta. Mr. Bright described Lord Beaconsfield in terms which we shall not repeat. Mr. Gladstone declared that the Royal prerogative on which the Prime Minister relied was a forgery. By other politicians, of a more advanced school, it was gravely asserted that Lord Beaconsfield entertained a fixed design of subverting the British Constitution with the help of Asiatic bayonets, and of restoring the Monarchy of the Stuarts in the person of Queen Victoria. It is needless to say that if there had been any serious objections to the employment of these forces such assertions would have smothered them in ridicule. But it was impossible to show that there was a single objection which was tenable. The people were greatly delighted with the sudden proof that England was a greater military power than they had supposed; and the effect which it produced on Russia and on all Europe was marked and instantaneous. The Opposition in Parliament, of course, did their worst. The measure, they said, was unconstitutional. The Queen had no such power. The people of India would be saddled with intolerable expenses. It was a violation of the India Bill of 1858; with much more to the same effect. But Lord Cairns in a single speech demolished the whole fabric of invective, and showed conclusively that both law and precedent were on the side of Ministers.

By this time the strength of Turkey had succumbed to her colossal foe, and a Treaty of Peace had been concluded by which English interests were very seriously threatened. The attitude of England, however, now induced Russia to pay serious attention to her remonstrances, and when Lord Beaconsfield insisted that the Treaty of San Stefano should be laid upon a European council table, Prince Gortschakoff, after much diplomatic fencing, the result of which was the Schouvaloff-Salisbury compromise, accepted Lord Beaconsfield's original proposal. The Congress of Berlin followed, and though considerable objections were taken at the time to the attendance of the Prime Minister himself as the representative of England, it is probable that there was no one else who could have made an equally strong impression on the Continental statesmen there assembled. The result of his mission was the memorable Treaty of Berlin, which will be for ever associated with his strenuous efforts to uphold what he believed to be the true interests of England.

It was the object of Lord Beaconsfield in the Treaty of Berlin to close against Russia the two approaches to the Mediterranean, and by occupying Cyprus to command her path through the Euphrates Valley. The efficacy of the means which he adopted has not yet been tested; and it would be premature to speak positively on the subject. It is sufficient to state that in London, after the signature of the Treaty, he was the hero of the hour; that the populace and the Parliament believed "peace with honour" to be no empty boast. Abroad, too, Lord Beaconsfield was thought to have achieved a still greater diplomatic triumph than he was credited with at home. The Austrian *Presse*, in particular, gave a summary of its results, from which we take the following remarks:—"The action of the British Cabinet since the signing of the Peace Treaty is now manifest. It tends to prove that, war or no war, the preponderance of English influence in Asia is henceforth secured. Egypt, with the Suez Canal and the maritime route to India, Asia Minor, with Arabia, as also Syria and the rich Euphrates district, Turkey on both sides the Bosphorus, together with the road over Persia to the vassal States of Central Asia, are now all under the powerful dominion of Great Britain. . . . Such is the great moral and political result not of the Berlin Congress, but of the course followed by the mighty Indo-British Empire, and which is henceforth to replace the old Anglo-Ottoman traditions and the old Russo-European views on the policy of the East." This was, however, an Austrian view of "England's triumph in the Eastern Question." But even at home the occupation of Cyprus, and the firm "Indo-British policy" which it signified, evoked general enthusiasm.

Immense majorities supported Lord Beaconsfield in Parliament. The Freedom of the City of London was conferred on him and on Lord Salisbury, and their progress from Parliament Street to Whitehall, on their return from Berlin, was one continued triumph. In the speech which he delivered after the subsequent banquet the Prime Minister gave as clear and concise an exposition of what he himself considered to be the real import of the Treaty as is anywhere to be found. The well-founded apprehensions which had prevailed both in this country and in Europe, he described as follows:—"That the balance of power in the Mediterranean might be subverted: that Russia might establish ports on the Ægean: that the restriction on the navigation of the Straits might be removed: that Asia Minor might be conquered: and the establishments and influence of Great Britain on the Persian Gulf might be seriously endangered:" and he claimed for the Treaty of Berlin that it had secured the best possible precautions against all these contingencies. Such for the time at least was thought to be the general opinion of the country, and when Parliament separated on the 16th of August there was no apparent reason to doubt that Lord Beaconsfield had every right to feel himself more secure than ever.

During the autumn of 1878 public attention was, however, diverted for a while from the Turkish

Question by the beginning of troubles in Afghanistan. But before these began to show themselves it was obvious that considerable difficulty would be experienced in carrying the Treaty of Berlin into execution. The populations whom it affected resisted the dispositions which had been made for them, and Greece in particular was exceedingly dissatisfied with the boundaries allotted her in the Treaty. But for the time all eyes were turned in a different direction; and for some months little or nothing was said of the progress of the Treaty towards completion. The short Afghan war of 1878 now belongs to history. It is sufficient to say that it was entirely successful; that we gained the "scientific frontier" declared to be imperatively necessary, not only by Lord Beaconsfield himself, but by the majority of experienced Indian statesmen, and that the war was concluded by a most satisfactory Treaty with the new Ameer, Yakoob Khan, in May, 1879. This was a success which it was impossible to deny or to explain away. The country was satisfied that Lord Beaconsfield had gauged the situation rightly, and that his action had been conformable to the traditional principles by which our Empire had been founded and preserved. What touched him more nearly were the assertions put forward by a portion of the London Press when the successful issue of our negotiations with Yakoob became known, to the effect that Russia's desertion of the

Afghans, which had contributed so largely to our success, had been purchased by concessions in Eastern Europe which virtually reduced the Treaty of Berlin to the level of the Treaty of San Stefano. Lord Beaconsfield, however, replied to this charge in a speech in the House of Lords in May, 1879, in which in a few incisive sentences he pointed out what the Treaty of San Stefano had proposed, and what the Treaty of Berlin had enacted, drawing out the contrast with a force and clearness which might have satisfied any reasonable mind.

With the spring of 1879 a fresh source of trouble developed itself in the affairs of South Africa, where it had seemed necessary to the High Commissioner, Sir Bartle Frere, to crush the military power of the Zulu King, Cetewayo, which he believed was a standing menace to the Colony. The Home Government was solicited for troops, which were sent out, though not without an intimation to Sir Bartle Frere that he was going faster than the Government desired. War, however, had now become inevitable, and crossing the frontier in false security, supposing that they had only a contemptible enemy to deal with, a portion of our forces was surrounded by the enemy, and cut off almost to a man.

One cry of grief and indignation resounded through the whole land. The miscarriage of our arms reflected on the Ministry, and the Government had to bear for a time the triple burden of an unexecuted Treaty of Berlin, a doubtful war in Afghanistan, and an unsuccessful one in South Africa. Lord Beaconsfield, however, was never greater than under misfortunes of this nature, and never carried himself more proudly than he did at this trying epoch. Presently, however, came the news that the evacuation of Roumelia by the Russians had begun, and that Yakoob Khan had submitted. The Government, which had certainly sunk somewhat in public estimation, regained its old level of popularity. And at this moment, when it could not be said that it was done under any pressure of public opinion, Sir Garnet Wolseley was sent out to South Africa to assume the chief political and military command.

The domestic policy of Lord Beaconsfield in 1879 was almost a blank. The fact is that the Government had done nearly as much as it could do in the existing Parliament. Two questions still remained which Government had been anxious to settle—the liability, namely, of employers for injuries sustained by their servants, and the reconstruction of our county administration. But on each of these questions Lord Beaconsfield was placed between two fires, and a General Election being at hand it was important not to run the risk of alienating any powerful body of his supporters. The Magistrates, generally speaking, were at issue on the subject of County Boards; employers and employed were at

issue as to the liability of the former. It would
have been unwise to give offence either to the
ratepayers, or the country gentlemen, or the railway companies, or the mill-owners, when their votes
were so shortly to be solicited; and these and other
measures gradually drifted out of sight.

One question, however, of great domestic interest
had risen to the surface during the winter and
spring of 1879, and that was the condition of
British agriculture. Commerce, no doubt, was
equally depressed; but the depression was common
to Europe; its causes were understood, and its revival confidently anticipated. That, however, was
not the case with the agricultural industries of this
country. They were, comparatively speaking, iso-
lated in their distress. Its causes were warmly
disputed, and its cure seemed doubtful and remote.
Foreign competition, however, had obviously a great
deal to do with it, and murmurs of Protection
accordingly began to make themselves audible in
Farmers' Clubs. It was under these circumstances
that the Marquis of Huntly called the attention
of the House of Lords to the subject, and inquired
whether Her Majesty's Government intended to
institute any inquiry into the causes of the prevailing suffering. This motion drew from Lord
Beaconsfield a remarkably able speech, in which he
declared once for all the impossibility of returning
to Protection, though not without reminding his

audience of what had been said upon the subject
"in another place, and in another generation." No
doubt he must have experienced some satisfaction,
what he himself would have called a "dismal con-
solation," in calling to the remembrance of the
public the warnings he had addressed during the
great commercial struggle which lasted from 1846
to 1850. The country, he said, had been warned
that if Protection was abandoned such at some
future time would be the inevitable consequences.
But the country deliberately decided to run the
risk. Two General Elections in succession afforded
ample opportunity for a reconsideration of the question had the public been so disposed. But the
Parliament of 1847 confirmed what had been done
in the two previous years, and the Parliament of
1852 confirmed what had been done afterwards.
For six years the country had been mainly occupied
with the consideration of the great question, and
the conclusion at which it finally arrived could not
lightly be tampered with. In the same speech he
pointed out, with great clearness, the effect upon
prices of the discovery of the gold-fields, of the
immense addition to the gold currency which was
suddenly created, and of the almost equally sudden
cessation of the Californian supply.

Before quitting the Session of 1879, however, we
may call attention to a motion brought forward on
the 13th of May in the Lower House by Mr.

Dillwyn, in which he sought to fasten upon the Government the charge to which we have before alluded, of reviving personal government, and withdrawing behind the veil of prerogative various public questions which ought to have been submitted to Parliament. The attempt broke down; for the very obvious reason that it was impossible to succeed in it without implicating the Sovereign, and it was impossible to produce any evidence to connect her with the practice complained of. But as a great deal was said at this time of Lord Beaconsfield's supposed view on the subject of the Royal Prerogative, it may not be amiss to explain what were his real ideas on the position of an English Sovereign. It is certain that the Revolution of 1688, when it once got into fair working order, supplied very substantial checks on the personal authority of a Prime Minister. The King could control him as he controlled Lord North and Mr. Pitt, and the aristocracy could control him through the machinery of the borough system, which lasted down to 1832. A Parliamentary majority, being largely composed of nominees, was always liable to be withdrawn, or, at least, seriously impaired, if the Minister ran counter to the wishes of the nobility. On the other hand, there was the Royal Prerogative, still further circumscribing the independence of the Premier. The Reform Bill, however, has effected a very great change in the position of the Prime Minister. It has emancipated him from the influence of the borough-monger, which was always at hand, and ready to act at a moment's notice. It has, to a great extent, freed him from the control of the Crown, if, as we are assured, no Sovereign could ever venture to dismiss Ministers who were supported by, or retain a Cabinet in defiance of, a majority of the House of Commons. And though this assertion may be somewhat in excess of the exact truth, it cannot be doubted that the power of the Crown to prevent a Minister with a majority from doing what he likes in Parliament, which was really possessed, to some extent, during the Georgian epoch, has now all but disappeared.

For these two checks, which, as we say, were immediate, instant, and direct, the Premier has now only to fear the unorganised and divided influence of public opinion acting at considerable intervals, and in the nature of things less curious about the privileges of Parliament and less jealous of the power of individuals than those who enjoy the one and are directly overshadowed by the other. The control of the aristocracy and the control of the Sovereign having both been virtually removed, the Prime Minister, if a man of commanding mind, is left virtually standing alone on a pinnacle of his own, under no control at all but the popular will. This was true of Mr. Gladstone, and is now true of him again; and, no doubt, it was true of Lord

Beaconsfield. The only difference is that the power of a modern Prime Minister is more precarious. Under the old *régime* when once a political Party got possession of power it was not very easy to dislodge it, and when its managers found a Minister to suit them they were in no hurry to get rid of him. Walpole held office twenty years, Lord North twelve; Pitt, Portland, Perceval, and, practically, Lord Liverpool, died in harness. It is improbable we shall ever see another Prime Minister holding office for a dozen years; but while he does hold it, he is more free to do as he likes than even Mr. Pitt was.

Now it is perfectly clear that when the Sovereign and the Prime Minister are in perfect accordance with each other, it is impossible to say which of them may exercise the power which has been actually intrusted to the latter. If a Statesman invested by the people with supreme power for seven years chooses to place it at the disposal of the Monarch, who shall say him nay? While if the Crown and the Minister shall not be in perfect harmony, it is obviously the former which must yield, unless the chance be preferred of trying an appeal to the country. As for withdrawing things from the cognisance of Parliament, that will depend a great deal on the position which Parliament occupies in public estimation. If a Minister finds that everything he does is exposed to factious, vexatious, and obstructive criticism, which is obviously condemned by public opinion out of doors, secure of that support it is very likely that he will be less ready to invite Parliamentary discussion than he otherwise might have been. The great reform of our Electoral system, which took place in 1867, has made it comparatively easy for him to avoid it. It has placed power in the hands of a class to whom Parliament is not all in all. The ordinary ratepayer is placed at too great a distance from the House of Commons to be as jealous for its supremacy as the middle and upper classes. More than forty years ago Lord Beaconsfield expressed in the House of Commons his distrust of a Monarchy of the middle classes. That he understood and made use of the Democratic tendency to place power in the hands of individuals is probably quite true, and to that extent the revival of Personal Rule may be connected with his name.

With the approach of the winter of 1879–80 public curiosity began to manifest itself as to the probability of a Dissolution of Parliament. But the Government gave no sign. Lord Mayor's-day came and went, and still no clue was afforded to the course which was likely to be adopted. It is possible that Lord Beaconsfield himself contemplated finishing a seventh Session of Parliament, and dissolving in the following autumn; considering that any objections which might be raised to this unusual prolongation of the existing Parliament would be more than compensated for by the chance of some improvement in the meantime taking place in the prospects of trade and agriculture.

The favourable results, however, of the Liverpool, Sheffield, and Southwark elections made such an impression on his colleagues, that they grew in favour of striking while the iron was hot; and a Dissolution was resolved upon in March. It was proclaimed by Lord Beaconsfield in a letter to the Lord-Lieutenant of Ireland, published on the 9th of March, in which the condition of Ireland, and the efforts of the Separatist Party were alleged to be the great subjects of national importance, though he also laid stress on the critical condition of Eastern Europe, and the necessity for consolidating English influence for the purpose of maintaining peace. Of Lord Beaconsfield's own anticipations conflicting accounts have been circulated. He certainly told the Lord Mayor that in all probability he should be addressing him again that time next year; but that might have meant very little. Nobody, however, was prepared for such a wholesale overthrow as that which occurred. The Conservative Party lost a hundred and eleven seats. The event is still much too recent to allow its significance to be justly gauged. Governments, like individuals, are liable to become stale. The distress of the country, both commercial and agricultural, was also a most important factor in producing the astonishing result. Add to these elements the effect of Mr. Gladstone's strictures on the Foreign Policy of the Government, and we have sufficient materials for explaining what occurred without supposing that the people were less Conservative than they were in 1874. That Lord Beaconsfield was mortified by the unexpected exhibition of popular caprice is undeniable, and he gave vent to his feelings in occasional cynical remarks on the little trust that could be reposed in the professions of the multitude. But, on the whole, the conduct of the Conservative Party and their illustrious leader under this unparalleled reverse was dignified and manly, and under his skilful counsel they speedily gained credit for a wise and patriotic attitude in their new position. His Lordship recommended them to reject the Compensation for Disturbance Bill, but he advised them, at the same time, to accept the Burials Bill and the Ground Game Bill, and to reserve their resisting power for more important and more dangerous proposals which he believed to be in store for us.

During the autumn of 1880 he remained very quiet, occupied probably with the revision of his new novel, which was published in the month of November. With the opening of Parliament in January, he was in his place, and apparently robust; and when seen in society nobody could have detected any sign of weakness or decay in him. Speaking on the Address on the 6th of

January, he delivered himself with all his accustomed force and felicity of expression, and laid special stress on the fact that the late Government had fully intended to renew the Peace Preservation Act; that their Bill was drawn; and that the measure itself, together with the important information on which it was founded, were placed at the service of their successors. They, however, considered such a measure to be unnecessary, and made themselves so far responsible for all the horrors which ensued. He spoke several times afterwards on Foreign Policy, more especially on India, and was scarcely ever more effective in his best days than in the recent debate on Lord Lytton's motion condemning the abandonment of Candahar. This was his last great speech in the Parliament he had so long adorned; nor could he have chosen a theme more suitable to mark the end of his illustrious career. Not, however, that this was his last service to his country. The advice which he tendered to the Constitutional party in the House of Commons on the change proposed by Mr. Gladstone in the mode of conducting public business was his final contribution to the cause of Parliamentary independence. Mr. Disraeli has always loved the House of Commons, and the House of Commons has returned his affection, his personal popularity in that Assembly having been second only to that of Lord Palmerston. In recommending the Leader of the

Opposition to resist the attempt of the Government to apply their new rules for silencing debate to the ordinary business of supply he showed his usual courage, and his usual zeal for the honour and credit of the House of Commons. Public opinion was unmistakably on his side, though whether the House has finally been saved from this complete destruction of its freedom still remains to be seen.

Of Mr. Disraeli as an orator we know not if any finished estimate has yet been written. But a brief comparison of his eloquence with that of his great rival may be expected in the present memoir. It has always seemed to us that Mr. Gladstone was strongest where Mr. Disraeli was weakest, and Mr. Disraeli strongest where Mr. Gladstone was weakest. The latter is clearly a type of the Peel school. Less cold and formal than Sir Robert, he appeals to essentially the same class of instincts in his countrymen. That is to say, he contrived for a long time to persuade both the City and the Church that he was their special representative. His eloquence has till lately been either of a sombre order, diffusing a "dim, religious light" all around him, or else business-like, statistical, and economical. Like Sir Robert Peel, he is a master of all ecclesiastical and financial subjects. And even in his very speeches we still detect the presence of that element of respectability which was a marked characteristic of Sir Robert. On finance alone do the spheres of Mr.

Gladstone and Mr. Disraeli touch one another. But on every other point they are wide asunder as the poles. As Mr. Gladstone—though with many points of difference—represents Peel, so Lord Beaconsfield, with many points of difference, represented Lord Palmerston—excelled where he excelled, and understood what he understood. His speeches, indeed, went far beyond those of Lord Palmerston in that mixture of sarcasm, cynicism, and *bonhomie* which is so thoroughly in harmony with the tone of English society, expressed with great felicity, and accommodated with consummate skill to the taste of his audience. There are touches of a second nature which makes the whole world of politics akin; and of these he was a perfect master. No one since Lord Palmerston could appeal so successfully from the severity of a senate to the more sportive tone of the club and the dinner-table. In speaking his delivery was inferior to Mr. Gladstone, who pours wave after wave of strong, idiomatic, albeit rather pallid, English upon the heads of his audience with a fluency that is wonderful. Lord Beaconsfield, on the contrary, used to hesitate a good deal, and seemed to have formed for himself a kind of reserve vocabulary on which he could always fall back when at a loss for words. The phraseology alluded to must be well-known to all his hearers; and indeed he had recourse to it so often latterly that it was fast running into mannerism. Lord

Palmerston likewise was always a hesitating speaker. Neither was Lord Beaconsfield at his very best when he was most serious; though some of his higher flights of eloquence have been incomparably good. He, moreover, had the art of extracting either novel or apparently novel propositions out of the most threadbare subjects, and though such power may be a snare to the statesman, it is a wonderful advantage to the orator, who is enabled thereby to invest his argument with ever-varying freshness and interest. But it is mainly, of course, on his sarcastic rhetoric and wealth of humorous illustration that his fame as a speaker will depend. Lord Beaconsfield, in fact, was almost the last representative of political wit —the wit of Carteret and Townsend, of North, Sheridan, and Canning, and, in a lesser degree, of the late Lord Derby and Lord Palmertson. This rare accomplishment was both his strength and his weakness. It occasionally tempted him into epigrams which he had better have kept to himself; while his brilliant audacity was so little in keeping with the decorous dulness of the House of Commons that it made men suspicious of his soundness. A vague idea that dulness and soundness go together is very prevalent among what we may call the Calico school of politicians; and no doubt for many of them it is a very consoling creed. But this unrivalled faculty gave Mr. Disraeli an immense influence with the intellectual public, while nothing could have served him better in his conflict with a class of minds, to be found perhaps on both sides of the House, whose prejudices are impervious to reason, but which dread wit as the brute creation dread fire. His brilliant and biting witticisms will live in the popular memory, as was said of Johnson's table-talk, long after his more elaborate and ornate compositions have become food for history.

Of Lord Beaconsfield as a man of letters something still remains to be said. We have already spoken of *Vivian Grey* and *Coningsby*, but rather from a political than a literary point of view. Lord Beaconsfield's novels, in fact, have always suffered from their political importance, since it has served in some degree to dwarf their dramatic excellence. It is far from improbable that had he not devoted to politics the mind so formed for literature, he might have rivalled our most eminent novelists. Posterity will determine whether he has not done so as it is. Whether we take the plot, the character, or the language, it would be difficult to name any work of fiction which is superior to *Coningsby* and *Sybil* on their own ground. Could we, indeed, name any one that has equalled them in the portraiture of those common-place characters to represent which faithfully is confessedly one of the highest triumphs of literary art? What Miss Austen has done for the country gentlemen and country clergymen, among whom she was brought up; what George Eliot has done for the farmers, the peasantry, and the tradesmen, whose peculiarities she had noted with an equally observant eye; that Lord Beaconsfield has done for the men of clubs and drawing-rooms, the political and social gossips, the Meltons and the Milfords, the Ormsbys and the Eskdales, who are as admirable in their way as the Bennets and the Eltons, the Poysers and the Tullivers of the two great artists we have mentioned. None but a great dramatic artist could reproduce such varying scenes and characters with such dazzling brilliancy. Nor is it only in this province of his art that he exhibits such pre-eminent ability. His descriptive power is in some respects unique. Take his picture of Wodgate or the burning of Mowbray Castle from *Sybil*, and those of Jerusalem and Fakradeen's Castle in the Lebanon from *Tancred*, and we challenge contradiction when we say they have never been surpassed since the author of *Waverley* and *The Talisman* was laid in the sepulchre of his ancestors. In *Lothair* and *Endymion* we have Lord Beaconsfield again endeavouring to disseminate political convictions through the medium of entertaining fiction, but in very unequal degrees. In *Lothair* the writer's purpose dominates over that of the mere novelist as much as in either *Sybil* or *Coningsby*. But in *Endymion* this is not so; and it may be read as a novel of society without our attention being drawn to its political character. In another department of literature Mr. Disraeli has likewise gained distinction. His *Life of Lord George Bentinck* is a political classic ; and contains many striking passages of eloquence, both grave and graphic.

It was the fashion at one time to speak of Lord Beaconsfield as a political adventurer. Yet there is no definition of an adventurer which will not include some of the most eminent names in the history of English politics. Is a political adventurer simply a man without a patrimony who makes politics a profession, as others do of law, divinity, or medicine? If so, then assuredly the two Pitts, Burke, Canning, and Macaulay were all political adventurers. Yet who with any political ambition would not rather have the reputation of any one of these than the reputation of Newcastle, Rockingham, Portland, or Liverpool? But is an adventurer a man without any aristocratical connections—a man born outside the charmed circle, who has to fight his way into it, if not by his "literature and his wit," by his eloquence and his perseverance? Again, we have the same names. And pre-eminently such men were Burke and Canning; such a man was Lord Beaconsfield, and such a man is Mr. Gladstone! Or, thirdly, is an adventurer a man who deserts a falling house, and always contrives, if possible, to be upon the winning side, who marches with every reaction just far enough to suit his purpose, and then stands aloof to be ready to take advantage of the next?

If this is the definition of an adventurer, we have certainly had such in our history, and at no distant date. But Lord Beaconsfield is not amongst them. He belonged to the class of professional politicians, like Burke, Pitt, and Canning, who all began life with slender means, and looked to politics to make their fortunes. But all three adhered steadily to the principles with which they entered public life, and Lord Beaconsfield has done the same. From the Reform Bill to the present day he has never once swerved from the views which he announced to the world in the *Vindication of the British Constitution*, and afterwards developed more fully in *Coningsby* and *Sybil*. To adhere unflinchingly for forty-five years to an unpopular and eccentric creed, which brings no political support, and is if anything a source of weakness, may be Quixotic, unpractical, fantastic, or what you like ; but assuredly it is not the mark of a political adventurer in the evil sense of that term. Lord Beaconsfield, like Burke, was not "rocked and dandled into a legislator." But it should be remembered that it was Burke who restored the moral existence of the Whigs. By his writings and his speeches he gave cohesion to those discordant cliques which made the first ten years of George III.'s reign a political chaos. He brought order out of this confusion, and reconstructed the Whig party on a popular and intelligible basis. This was the work of one political adventurer, unless we fix an arbitrary meaning on the word to suit our own occasions. Mr. Pitt, again, was certainly the son of an earl, but though that gave him an introduction to political life, it gave him nothing else. His elder brother could do nothing for him, and when he entered Parliament as the pupil of Lord Shelburne he must undoubtedly have looked forward to making a livelihood by politics. Yet this was the man who did for the Tory party all, and far more than all, that Burke had accomplished for the Whigs—raised it from the ground, gave it a new meaning and a new vitality, and started it on a triumphant career which endured for nearly half a century. Again, from 1822 to 1826, it was Canning, the adventurer, "the writing fellow," who won for the Tory party all the popularity it possessed, and who, had he lived, would have saved it from the blunders of the Duke of Wellington, and from the long-continued effects of the vacillating policy of Peel. The real re-constructor of the Tory party, since 1832 is Lord Beaconsfield, who in his turn has been styled an "adventurer." But he is distinctly no more of an adventurer than the other distinguished men to whom, in succession, the two great parties in the State have been so deeply indebted.

Lord Beaconsfield lived so thoroughly in politics that little remains to be said of his private or domestic life. He was a man of very kind and genial nature; particularly fond of children, and though addicted to silence, was not remarkable for reserve. At his own table he desired others to talk rather than himself; and if he caught a remark which seemed to possess any merit, he would immediately call attention to it, and take care that it was properly appreciated. His style of living was comparatively simple, and at Hughenden, though he and Lady Beaconsfield took great delight in the beautiful woods which surrounded them, there was no appliances for field sports. Lord Beaconsfield neither kept hunters nor preserved game, leaving it to his tenants to supply him at their own discretion. But he felt all a politician's interests in the Chiltern Hills, and was fond of driving among them with an appreciative stranger, showing him Great Hampden and Chequers Court, and repeating anecdotes of the Great Rebellion, which, he used to say, was hatched in these recesses. The Chiltern Hills are rich in natural beauty and historic associations. But neither their green glades nor their ancient mansions will yield anything in future more attractive or interesting to the tourist than the picturesque old Manor House henceforth and for ever to be associated with the name of Beaconsfield.

Lord Beaconsfield, be his defects of character and errors of conduct what they may, will be remembered among the great "Parliament men" whom this country has produced, and whose renown is the common property of Englishmen. For nearly three centuries Parliamentary Government in England has developed a succession of orators, adminstrators, and leaders of parties the like of whom' no other nation can boast. From the sturdy patriots of Queen Elizabeth's reign down through the struggles with the Stuarts, the Long Parliament and the Great Rebellion, the Restoration and the Revolution, English Constitutional statesmanship was nurtured and trained for its "flowering period," which began with Bolingbroke and Walpole, and, we rejoice to believe, is not yet near its close. How many among the most splendid illustrations of that portion of our annals will history place higher than Lord Beaconsfield? It is idle to mete out honour by strict rule and measure. Lord Beaconsfield, as all must acknowledge, was an almost unique character, and that he differed in almost every intellectual quality from his predecessors was patent throughout his remarkable career.

Nor is Lord Beaconsfield's fame of that kind which will be seriously impaired by lapse of time. A statesman may do good service to his country, and his work may remain behind him, and yet the personality of the man may quickly fade away, and the labours he achieved may sink into the common stock of national acquisitions, and excite no emotional movements of gratitude. But it was given to Lord Beaconsfield to colour the political life of England for an entire generation, and even in his old age—as the deep and general interest excited by his illness proves—his influence upon the popular imagination was paramount. It will not be possible during the lifetime of those who felt that influence—whether in the form of attraction or repulsion—to estimate justly the political results of Lord Beaconsfield's statesmanship. But those who have known him and who feel keenly what a change his death has made in the atmosphere of English politics are better able than the most dispassionate of judges, and the most ruthless of critics, to bear testimony to the effect produced on followers and opponents alike by the peculiar genius of the late Chief of the Conservative Party.

The career of Mr. Disraeli, to speak of Lord Beaconsfield by the name identified with his greatest efforts, may be contemplated from many different points of view. As a statesman devoted to principles, and bent on applying them in action, and as the leader of a party defeated and disorganised repeatedly, and raised under his admirable guidance to a position of strength and good repute, Mr. Disraeli made a name for himself, the lustre of which no rancorous efforts of political partisanship can darken. The title of Lord Beaconsfield is chiefly associated in our minds with the late Adminstration, and with the critical questions of Foreign Policy which disturbed the public mind on the approach of the last General Election.

But our memory of Mr. Disraeli goes back rather to the days when he was contending against superior numbers, and an apparently unconquerable mass of popular prejudice, at the head of the Conservative Party in the House of Commons. When the Government of Sir Robert Peel was shattered by the Free Trade controversy, and the Protectionists were organised as a separate party, the Leadership in the House of Commons fell almost inevitably to Mr. Disraeli, and that office he filled for nearly thirty years, occasionally in office, more usually in Opposition, and only during the last couple of years —from 1874 to 1876, when he was elevated to the peerage—really wielding the power of a Minister with a large and obedient majority at his command. Throughout those days of adversity, when the Conservative Party were seldom cheered by a ray of hope, Mr. Disraeli showed himself a master of almost every form of Parliamentary ability, and, in spite of jealousy, of intrigue, and of a continuous hail of slanders, he got himself recognised not only as the indispensable leader of the Conservatives, but as one of the foremost and most characteristic representatives of the House of Commons.

It has often been said, with what degree of truth it is not necessary to inquire, that Mr. Disraeli's origin and mental bias unfitted him to represent, and even to understand, the semi-articulate wishes of the English people. But in a more limited sphere Mr.

Disraeli succeeded beyond all doubt in representing and assimilating English feeling. Few statesmen in modern times have so thoroughly understood the House of Commons, have been so careful of its dignity and honour, so reverential towards its great traditions, and so faithful to its prevailing spirit. We do not refer, of course, to matters of policy in which Mr. Disraeli found the majority generally opposed to him; we speak rather of the manner in which he conducted public business, whether as head of the Government or as Leader of the Opposition.

The same indomitable perseverance and undaunted valour with which he fought the battle of his party against overwhelming odds and apparently hopeless destinies might have served his country hereafter on a larger theatre, and in the cause of more extended interests. His whole career, with the exception of the few short years of power which marked its close, is one long illustration of this remarkable characteristic. His literary reputation was established at a single stroke, and ran on very different lines from the difficult and laborious path by which he climbed to political eminence. But his first appearance in the House of Commons, and a failure more famous than many triumphs, form but the fitting introduction to a public life of singular vicissitudes, surmounted one after the other by the same intrepid spirit which forty-four years ago told the Parliament of England that they should still listen to him. How from this unpromising commencement he gradually rose to be the foremost man of the party to which he had attached himself: and the successive steps by which he led his party to victory after a series of reverses which would have crushed any ordinary statesman, it will be for his biographer to relate. It is sufficient to point out the remarkable fact that though he has required from his followers as large sacrifices as any of his predecessors, he yet never forfeited their support, and that to the last day of his life, when the leader once again of a vanquished and disheartened minority, he was regarded with as much veneration as he had ever commanded in his most brilliant and triumphant moments.

The European estimate of Lord Beaconsfield was indicated in the telegrams published the day after his death from the different Continental capitals. That the impression produced by his death should be only less profound abroad than at home was, indeed, to be expected. In Paris, Vienna, Berlin, and in all other chief centres of European thought and action, he had long been something more than the leader of a great political party. There, as in England, he enjoyed two distinct kinds of fame. The brilliancy of his parts, and the lustre of his purely intellectual achievements, exercised an irresistible fascination, long before his power and *prestige* as a statesman were felt. More justice, perhaps, has been done to Lord Beaconsfield, as the master of a literary style whose epigrammatic flavour is almost unique, by the cultivated critics of the Continent than by his own countrymen. They have long recognised in him a writer and speaker entitled to the largest measure of cosmopolitan fame. The very fact of his lineage, and of the obstacle which it seemed to interpose in the path of his advancement, invested his career and his success with a richer and more piquant attraction in foreign eyes. His books had been translated into every language of the Western world, and had been commented upon in the literary reviews of every capital. He had achieved a high place in that great republic of intellect which knows no distinction of nationality or climate. His genius, with all its profoundly interesting qualities, was felt long ere his capacities in international statesmanship and diplomacy had made themselves known.

When, therefore, Lord Beaconsfield went to Berlin, three years ago, he was infinitely less of a stranger to the Continental public than the two or three of his political contemporaries who vied with him in national reputation. He had for years been regarded as a European personage. There was much curious speculation as to how far he was qualified to take rank as a European force. Lord Beaconsfield did not disappoint the expectations to which the news of his approaching presence in the German capital gave rise. He fulfilled the great idea that had been formed of him. He took his place with every mark of honour at the table round which the Plenipotentiaries of the Great Powers were gathered. His bearing, his manner, his speech, powerfully impressed all those who were brought into contact with him. Our Berlin correspondent tells us that Prince Bismarck has been personally touched by the tidings of Lord Beaconsfield's death. Nor can we forget that during the summer of 1878 the Imperial Chancellor expressed his appreciation of Lord Beaconsfield's qualities with unmistakable sincerity. Independently of the political results of the Berlin Congress, no one can doubt that the impression which the statesman who was then Prime Minister of England stamped on the minds of the representatives of Europe, and on the opinion of Europe generally, was both vivid and permanent.

Long before Lord Beaconsfield arrived in Berlin, he was looked upon by every section of Continental critics as the statesman who had displayed a greater fidelity to the traditional spirit of England than any Prime Minister since the days of Palmerston. The memory of this incident naturally colours, and with evident diversity of hue, the remarks of the Russian, the German, and the Austrian press on Lord Beaconsfield's death. It signalised a great step taken in the direction of co-operation with Austria and Germany against Russian aggression.

An able and interesting article in the *Débats* described, with remarkable felicity and correctness, the part played by Lord Beaconsfield in the sphere of domestic politics. He was spoken of as "the representative of that non-exclusive Toryism which has enabled the aristocracy of England to remain Liberal without ceasing to be Conservative." The statement has more to recommend it than its antithetical shape. As the great idea of Lord Beaconsfield abroad was to prevent the old *Civis Romanus sum* doctrine from becoming obsolete, and to secure for the British Empire the exercise of Imperial authority, so did he at home incessantly aim at widening—and by widening, deepening—the foundation of Conservatism as a political faith and a national force. Who, he again and again asks in his writings, are the friends of the people if not the Tory party? There may seem an air of historic paradox about the proposition which the inquiry conveys, but when Lord Beaconsfield spoke of Toryism in its relation to the masses, he did not always use the words in their conventional sense. It is certain that he was always loyal to his own interpretation of the principles of Toryism, and that nothing was further from his thoughts than deliberately to resist the declared wish of the English people. "Do by legislation what in other countries is done by revolution," might perhaps be cited as the sum and substance of his notions as to the active mission of the Conservative party. This explains much of the influence he exercised over his followers in Parliament and in the nation at large, whilst a general consciousness of the fact is shown by the deep emotion which his death has elicited in all parts of the country, and among all conditions of the English people.

But the telegrams which appeared in *The Standard*, April 20, showed that something more was deplored than the death even of a great statesman and a great patriot. Lord Beaconsfield possessed qualities such as few public men have ever shown, and such as irresistibly won the respect and admiration of Englishmen. He personified a higher principle than that of mere personal success; and the story of his career is the eloquent record of great services. No mental equipment, however splendid, no combination of external circumstances, however auspicious, would have sufficed to raise him to the pinnacle of greatness which he attained, unless they had been accompanied by other attributes. Lord Beaconsfield always exhibited and always practised inexhaustible patience and infinite fortitude. He was a formidable foe, but his enmity was always open and honourable. He was effective in Opposition, yet he was never vexatious or factious. He gradually reached the highest office which a subject can occupy, because he possessed, and because he systematically used, those gifts of sagacity and courage without some proportion of which no success, even upon a lowlier level of life, is to be commanded. He bore himself with composure and dignity under the most bitter political reverses, and the temper which he has consistently manifested since the General Election of a year ago has materially added to his reputation among his countrymen.

## II.

### THE LAST ILLNESS.

It was on Wednesday, March 23, 1881, that the public first became aware that Lord Beaconsfield was not in the enjoyment of his usual health. On that day there appeared in *The Standard* this paragraph: "The Earl of Beaconsfield, who is suffering from a slight cold, was considerably better yesterday. Although the noble Earl did not go out during the day, he transacted business almost as usual. Dr. Kidd called upon his Lordship in the course of the morning, but there is nothing at all serious in his indisposition." As was natural, comparatively little anxiety was caused by this announcement, and nothing further was said on the subject till six days later, March 29, on the morning of which day these lines were published:—"The attack of bronchial asthma from which Lord Beaconsfield has been suffering was very severe, and was at one time a real cause of anxiety to his friends. Dr. Kidd remained with him the whole of Sunday night. A favourable change took place yesterday, and the gout has come out well, to the relief of the asthma."

As soon as it became known that Lord Beaconsfield's malady was not merely a passing cold, but a serious attack of bronchitis complicated with gout, public alarm became fully aroused, and numerous inquiries began to be made at his residence in Curzon Street. At nine o'clock in the morning of Tuesday, March 29, Dr. Kidd, Lord Beaconsfield's ordinary medical attendant, who had considered it necessary to remain at the house during the night, left Curzon Street, after issuing the following bulletin:—"Lord Beaconsfield had a restless night, partly through the pain of gout. The paroxysm of asthma less severe but frequent." The publication of this report in the evening papers by no means tended to diminish the apprehensions which the morning's announcement had excited. A copy of it was at once sent to the Queen at Buckingham Palace, and Her Majesty having expressed a wish that a consultation should be held, Dr. Quain was sent for, and, after a careful inquiry into Lord Beaconsfield's symptoms, he came to the conclusion that his Lordship was suffering from bronchitic asthma, complicated with gout. He expressed his entire approval of the treatment adopted by Dr. Kidd, and arranged to meet him again at ten o'clock in the evening. Before leaving the house at four in the afternoon, Dr. Quain wrote a bulletin to the following effect :—" Lord Beaconsfield has been free from spasmodic attack during the day, and his Lordship's strength has been fully maintained."

While the doctors were in consultation Mr. Gladstone walked to Curzon Street from Downing Street and had an interview with Lord Barrington, who was from the first, and remained till the last, in attendance upon Lord Beaconsfield. During the afternoon and evening there was a constant succession of visitors at the house, amongst whom were the Duke and Duchess of Connaught, the Duke of Cambridge, and many of the leading members of both political parties. At ten o'clock another consultation was held between Dr. Quain and Dr. Kidd. They reported that Lord Beaconsfield had been undisturbed by spasmodic attacks during the evening; that he was rather more feverish; but that in other respects his symptoms were not more unfavourable. Shortly after Dr. Quain left an official announcement was made as follows :—" Lord Beaconsfield's health during the evening has been undisturbed by spasms. His Lordship is suffering less, and he has been able to take nourishment." Dr. Kidd remained with Lord Beaconsfield all night.

The impression produced by the knowledge that Lord Beaconsfield's indisposition was serious may be judged from the following leading article in *The Standard* of March 30 :—" The news of Lord Beaconsfield's illness has been received by every section of

[Margin: March 29]

the public with deep concern and regret. The latest bulletins justify the hope that we shall soon hear of his approaching convalescence, but the severity of the present attack has not yet abated, and the weather which we are now having, invigorating as it may be to the young and strong, must sharply tax the most robust constitutions that have completed their seventh decade. For a few days to come the health of the Conservative leader will be a matter of anxiety, though not, we still trust, one of serious apprehension to the nation.

"For it is the whole English nation, and not any one particular division or party of it, which hopes that Lord Beaconsfield may speedily be restored to his normal health and vigour. In this country differences of political opinion are not inscribed in characters of abiding personal embitterment, and the sentiments to which, as Conservatives, we now give utterance will touch a sympathetic chord which will be responded to equally by those who do not belong to the same school of political thought as ourselves. In England, slightly to alter Macaulay's happy phrase, the shrine of reconciliation is reached much earlier than the temple of silence. As yet our political life is untainted by the contagion of personal animosities, and the most loyal of private friends may be the most uncompromising of public enemies. If this be true in the case of men who are actively engaged in party struggles, it is even more true of the English people at large. There are no critics so just, so impartial, and at the same time so generous as those who are personally unknown to the illustrious subject of their remarks.

"To-day it is Lord Beaconsfield; a few months ago it was Mr. Gladstone. The mass of Englishmen do not, when they learn that one in whom they recognise a national leader is in physical suffering, and it may be peril, ask themselves whether he has or has not consistently represented what they may happen to think are their own political views. They judge him by his achievements and his merits, by the standard of his public services, by the general calibre and consistency of his whole career. In the complex system of our public life there may be found—such is the view of the English public— an ample place for every sort of excellence. We may be living under what we are told is a Democracy, and perhaps that Democracy may at times appear somewhat mutable. But if it is periodically capricious, it is permanently appreciative. The qualities of greatness and devotion to public affairs never fail to secure their true measure of national recognition. The constituencies change their political humour, but the canons by which they judge of political greatness and deserts are fixed and unaltered. It is at such conjunctures as the present, when one of the most illustrious Englishmen of his epoch is the victim of a fatiguing and anxious malady, that words which would at ordinary times be trite and conventional acquire a fresh reality.

"Less than a year has passed since Lord Beaconsfield was Prime Minister. The position which he now fills, in point of honour and influence, is subordinate only to that of the Premier himself. The First Lord of the Treasury and the Leader of her Majesty's Opposition are the two great terms in the equation of political power in England. The one can as little be an irresponsible statesman as the other. No one has ever shown a deeper conviction of this truth than Lord Beaconsfield, nor is there any other respect than this in which his mere political superiority to Mr. Gladstone has more conspicuously made itself felt. Since the General Election of last year he has shown this sense of having a reversionary interest in the exercise of official power, which has commanded the admiration of his most persistent political opponents. It is good for public men to magnify their apostleship; it is on every account desirable that the leader of the attacks made upon a Government should appreciate, from experience, what the onerous functions of Government are.

"In no other country of the world does the Prime Minister fill anything like the same place which he occupies here. In most European States the office can scarcely be said to exist, for the simple reason that genuine representative government is unknown.

In France, in Italy, and in Spain, the Premier is only the chief of a victorious party, or the creature of political convenience. Probably one of the reasons which at the present moment renders M. Gambetta averse to accept the succession to M. Jules Ferry is that the President of the Chamber knows that in doing so he would derogate from his own dignity by identifying himself with a particular faction. The English Prime Minister must, it is true, be a party man. But he must be something more. He must actively discharge many of the duties which essentially appertain to Sovereignty. He cannot divest himself of the consciousness that he appears on various occasions as the direct representative of the Monarchy. It is this feeling which gives gravity and dignity to the office, and which causes the Prime Minister of England to rise above the level that satisfies the politicians who fill an analogous office elsewhere.

"No First Lord of the Treasury has ever shown a more chivalrous conviction of this fact than Lord Beaconsfield. The same spirit which he has manifested in power he has illustrated in Opposition. He has regarded his functions as charged with the same responsibility whether he happened to sit on the right hand or the left hand of the Speaker, or of the Lord Chancellor. In the Upper Chamber of the Legislature this feeling has, perhaps, been intensified by the knowledge that he has there a majority at his command. Hence it is that he has always filled, and that he continues to fill, a larger place in the public mind than ever perhaps before fell to the lot of the Leader of her Majesty's Opposition. His steady and consistent purpose has been so to conduct himself in Opposition that he might approach the place of power with dignity and without embarrassment.

"In one respect the illness of Lord Beaconsfield is calculated to point the same moral as did that of Mr. Gladstone a year ago. The age may be a levelling one; but democracy brings with it its own compensations. The rule of numbers will never exclude the supremacy of individuals, and the destinies of the multitude will continue to be controlled by those whom a contemporary critic has called 'exaggerated personalities.' Lord Beaconsfield and Mr. Gladstone are incomparably the two most distinguished public men of our epoch. Their national services are great; their political calibre is unapproached by any one of their contemporaries. If the English people felt this last summer, when Mr. Gladstone lay sick in Downing Street, they will feel it more now when they read the bulletins issued from Lord Beaconsfield's house in Mayfair.

"Mr. Gladstone has been successful in proportion as he has identified himself with great popular movements, and as a statesman he has almost retired into obscurity when the tide has turned against him. This has never been the case with Lord Beaconsfield.

The Leader of her Majesty's Opposition has achieved the same place in the scale of national opinion as the Prime Minister by dint of consummate political management. He has relied not upon the propulsive power of the multitude, but upon the patient strategy of statesmanship, and he has displayed qualities in this work which Englishmen will never cease to admire, and of which his illustrious rival has given no trace. He has not only trod the up-hill path of an opposed career; he has been voted to the Leadership of a great political party by something better than acclamation—by conviction. He has had able colleagues and loyal followers.

"Capacity of political criticism is no Liberal monopoly. It exists as much on one side of the House of Commons as the other. Lord Beaconsfield could never have led his party to victory without showing them, in the face of many obstacles, that he possessed the true attributes of the leader—the energy, the conviction, the earnestness were there. What was wanted was the concentration of force. Lord Beaconsfield called no such agency for the first time into existence, but he brought all of them, so to speak, to a definite focus. During many years he showed how this power was to be turned to lasting account, and gradually he succeeded in transforming a political minority into a majority. Mr. Gladstone never attempted anything of this kind, and had he done so he would have failed. Englishmen are not likely to forget this difference between the two Leaders, and the more it is remembered and realised, the greater is the *prestige* which will be conferred upon the career of Lord Beaconsfield."

In the course of Wednesday, March 30, Lord Beaconsfield's condition did not improve. The bulletin issued in the morning of that day was indeed hopeful:—" Lord Beaconsfield's spasmodic attacks have been less frequent during the night, and his Lordship is less exhausted than he was in the earlier part of yesterday." In reply to inquiries, Dr. Quain intimated that this bulletin did not signify that Lord Beaconsfield was to be considered out of danger, though there was a marked improvement in his condition. His Lordship had, during the night, been able to take nourishment, and when his physicians paid their early visit he was in good spirits.

Dr. Kidd left the house between ten and eleven o'clock in the morning, and did not return until half-past four, when he only remained a few minutes, coming back an hour later. As no bulletin was issued, it was understood that the symptoms were favourable, but it subsequently transpired that Lord Beaconsfield had not passed a good day, and that he was so much weaker in the evening as to cause his medical attendants considerable anxiety.

At ten o'clock on Wednesday night, March 30,

Dr. Quain again arrived, and, after visiting his Lordship, held another long consultation with Dr. Kidd the result of which was the following bulletin:—
"Lord Beaconsfield has had several attacks of spasmodic breathing during the day, and his Lordship is scarcely as well as he was in the morning." This bulletin was, as the others preceding it had been, at once forwarded to her Majesty and the other members of the Royal Family.

The number of visitors in Curzon Street throughout the day was very great, and plainly indicated how deep and widespread was the public sympathy with Lord Beaconsfield in his serious condition. Over 700 names were inscribed in the visitors' book, while in the afternoon the carriages were at times six or seven deep, waiting for their occupants to see the latest bulletin.

Again it may be well to indicate the interest taken in Lord Beaconsfield's state by giving some extracts from a leading article which appeared in *The Standard* on the following day:—"The public will learn with regret that Lord Beaconsfield is not progressing so satisfactorily as it was hoped he would do. The best evidence of the public solicitude caused by Lord Beaconsfield's illness is to be found in the list of those who called yesterday and the day before to make inquiries in Curzon Street. We had to publish just such another catalogue when Mr. Gladstone was confined to his bed in Downing Street last summer. The

Prime Minister has reciprocated in a specially attentive manner the tribute of courteous concern of which he was himself then the recipient from the Leader of her Majesty's Opposition. All the chief members of the Government and supporters of the Ministry have done the same thing. The number of those who have written their names in the visiting-book is not confined to statesmen and politicians, but includes the representatives of every class of the community. From the Royal Family down to the artisan, the private house of the Conservative Leader is the chief centre of personal interest, and the first glance, when the newspaper is unfolded this morning, will be to the column which contains the latest accounts of Lord Beaconsfield's health.

"The statesman who did not recognise in such testimonies of patriotic concern one of the solaces for the vexation of spirit and weariness of public life would be strangely callous and cynical. As a matter of fact, we know very well that the men who are the objects of this national affection and regard gratefully appreciate them at their true worth. Mr. Gladstone acknowledged the kindly feeling shown towards him on all sides in a letter which was at once graceful, felicitous, and pathetic. Lord Beaconsfield will not be less deeply impressed. A career of incessant devotion to public affairs does not blunt or dull the capacity of human sensitiveness on such occasions as the present. In a famous and eloquent passage, Lord Beaconsfield has described how intolerable would be the lot of the public man if he could not count in the long run upon popular forbearance and sympathy. Lord Beaconsfield has always shown remarkable accuracy—an accuracy for which mere shrewdness without imagination would be unable to account—in his estimate of English character. The English people, he has said repeatedly, are the most emotional and enthusiastic of the world; 'they conceal under a vest of pride more than foreigners show with their recklessness of histrionic display.'

"This opinion is receiving its justification now in a way that Lord Beaconsfield himself would, perhaps, scarcely have contemplated. The Leader of the Conservative Party has never condescended to be a hunter after such popularity. Some people think that he has too studiously avoided all appearances in the *rôle* of the popular statesman. He has never been addicted to field sports. He has never shown himself unnecessarily among the multitude. Few politicians of any eminence have exercised such reserve in the matter of attending public meetings. He has engaged most sparingly in promiscuous correspondence, and the position which he has occupied among his friends and colleagues has often been one of detachment and even isolation. 'After all,' Lord Beaconsfield has observed of the younger Pitt, 'a man who is Prime Minister at twenty-five cannot wear his heart on his sleeve.' Lord Beaconsfield was not Prime Minister till between thirty and forty years later. But much of the reserve which was characteristic of the son of Chatham has uniformly marked his public and his private demeanour.

"This is not the bearing by which a public man is usually supposed to endear himself to the multitude; and Lord Beaconsfield has never been a popular favourite in the sense in which Lord Palmerston was. But the English people are capable of being impressed in more ways than one. They like *bonhomie* in the great; they love to know that Prime Ministers or Secretaries of State are men of like passions with themselves; they delight in recognising illustrious personages at Epsom Downs on Derby-day. But they can also be profoundly affected, as the result has shown, by the spectacle of self-contained resolution and disciplined capacity pressing on steadily and surely to the supreme goal. The place occupied by Lord Beaconsfield in English politics is altogether unique. There is a quality in his genius which no other English statesman has ever shown. His determination, his patience, his masterly self-control, his incessant vigilance and effort, his never-failing recognition of the true opportunity, and his extraordinary skill in turning it to account; these are attributes which have appealed to the imagination of Englishmen.

"A sincere hope everywhere exists that this illness will rapidly take a favourable turn, and that before long Lord Beaconsfield will appear in his accustomed place in Parliament, full of renewed vigour and vitality. The age of statesmen is not to be reckoned by the calendar alone. Both the Prime Minister and the Leader of the Opposition have more than completed their threescore years and ten. But it never occurs to any one to speak of either as having completed his work. English public men are in the habit of dying in harness, and the expiring effort of Chatham in the House of Lords is an historical incident which has all the significance of a typical allegory. The business of the world is carried on by 'Sovereigns and Statesmen,' and, with almost the single exception of M. Gambetta, the chief makers of history in every country of Europe at the present moment are well advanced in years. Since the days of Canning no English Prime Minister has gone to an early grave, and even Canning, though Lord Lyndhurst once spoke of him as a boy, lacked but three years of threescore. Palmerston, Derby, Russell were each of them aged men; Lyndhurst himself delivered one of the greatest speeches which has ever been heard in the Upper House when he was close on eighty-four; and Englishmen still hope for much from Lord Beaconsfield."

On Thursday there appeared to be an improvement in Lord Beaconsfield's condition. Dr. Kidd, as on the previous evenings of the week, spent the night of Wednesday with his distinguished patient. During its earlier hours Lord Beaconsfield was extremely restless, and had several fits of coughing, but he gradually became more composed, and after taking some slight nourishment fell into a quiet sleep in the morning. Dr. Quain again arrived at the house at half-past nine, and three-quarters of an hour later, after another consultation, the physicians issued the following bulletin :—" Lord Beaconsfield has passed a quieter night, and his Lordship's condition is no worse this morning." After the physicians had left Curzon Street in the morning Lord Beaconsfield again fell into a quiet slumber, and on awakening appeared refreshed, and was able to take some nourishment. Shortly after four o'clock Dr. Kidd returned, and remained at the house for nearly two hours. Lord Beaconsfield was removed from the bedroom he had previously occupied to the back drawing-room, a much larger apartment. Dr. Quain and Dr. Kidd again visited the house at nine o'clock in the evening, and at a quarter to ten the following bulletin was issued :—" Lord Beaconsfield has passed a quiet day, and his Lordship's symptoms are rather more favourable."

April 1. On Thursday night Lord Beaconsfield was able to obtain some refreshing sleep. Dr. Quain arrived at Curzon Street at half-past nine o'clock on the morning of Friday, April 1, and had a consultation with Dr. Kidd, with the result that at ten o'clock this bulletin appeared:—" Lord Beaconsfield has passed the night without any severe attack of spasm. His Lordship is weak, but in other respects his symptoms are improved." Lord Beaconsfield was now able to take some substantial food, and after the doctors had left the house he fell into a gentle slumber. As perfect quiet was considered essential, and it was found that the noise of the vehicles in the street penetrated as far as the sick room, straw was laid down in the roadway. This effectually deadened the sound of passing carriages, and no one except the two nurses saw the patient until the afternoon. Dr. Kidd returned to the house after an absence of four hours, at a little before three o'clock, and remained some time, the verbal report after his departure being to the effect that Lord Beaconsfield's condition remained unchanged. About this time he became more restless, and a development of gout in the foot which had not hitherto been affected caused a certain degree of feverishness. The second consultation of the day took place at nine o'clock, and lasted for nearly an hour and a half. The following was the bulletin:—Lord Beaconsfield has been more restless and feverish during the afternoon—a result due in some measure to the development of gout in the foot which has not been hitherto affected." During the day a telegram was received by Lord Barrington from Lord Rowton to the effect that he was detained at Marseilles by his sister's illness, and that the doctors forbade him to leave her.

April 2. Throughout Friday night Dr. Kidd remained in attendance upon Lord Beaconsfield, who slept fairly well and was able to take nourishment. Dr. Quain returned at half-past nine in the morning, and this was the bulletin:—" Lord Beaconsfield has had some quiet sleep during the night. The gout in the right foot is rather more developed. The spasms have been relieved, otherwise the chest symptoms continue much the same." It was considered by the physicians that the patient had exerted himself too much during the previous day, and the strictest injunctions were therefore given that he should see no one beyond his personal attendants, and that the utmost silence should be maintained in the house and neighbourhood, so as to allow him to sleep, if possible. In consequence of this, even Lord Barrington and Sir Philip Rose, who had been constant in their attendance, abstained from visiting Lord Beaconsfield, and in the evening when the physicians held their second consultation they were able to issue the following report:—"Lord Beaconsfield has had some quiet hours of sleep at intervals during the day. He has been altogether free from spasmodic attacks since morning. His Lordship is weak, but has had no increase of

## THE LAST ILLNESS. 101

weakness during the day." On Sunday, April 3, after the usual morning visit of Dr. Quain, the most satisfactory bulletin that had appeared for two days appeared:—" Lord Beaconsfield has had a comparatively quiet night, the attacks of spasms being few and slight. In other respects his Lordship's condition is favourable and his strength maintained."

At noon, however, Lord Beaconsfield was again seized by a spasmodic attack, and both the doctors were speedily called in. A report of this relapse soon spread, and caused considerable alarm. But the reassuring announcement came shortly afterwards that his Lordship had quite recovered from the seizure, and had fallen into a sound slumber. This sleep lasted for over an hour, and when the physicians paid their afternoon visit they found the condition of the invalid to be so favourable as to justify their not issuing a second bulletin.

They were again at Curzon Street at nine o'clock, and after a consultation of nearly an hour's duration another bulletin was posted in the following terms:—" At noon to-day Lord Beaconsfield had a return of spasm, by which he was depressed for some hours. Since then his Lordship has had some sleep and nourishment, and is not materially worse than he was in the morning." After issuing this, Dr. Quain left the house, but Dr. Kidd remained for the night. In addition to the official report the doctors admitted that the return of the spasmodic attacks caused them much anxiety. In face of the severe north-east wind which prevailed it was declared to be very difficult to combat these symptoms. The patient's room was maintained at a temperature of 64 to 65 degrees, and bronchitis kettles were kept at work to secure the necessary dampness of the atmosphere.

April 4. Lord Beaconsfield's condition was obviously the more precarious because his malady, unlike some acute diseases, was not one which could be expected to run a definite course to a termination fatal or unfavourable. Thus, for instance, the earlier part of Monday, April 4, afforded much encouragement to those who watched by the bedside of the patient, and the best hopes were entertained; but at night the physicians recognised the presence of an increase of fever, which, though slight, could not but cause anxiety. The most satisfactory feature of the case was that there had as yet been no failure of strength. For the eighth night in succession Dr. Kidd remained with his Lordship, and on Monday morning, shortly after nine o'clock, he was joined by Dr. Quain and by a new physician, Dr. Bruce. The result of the consultation was the issue of the following bulletin:—"Lord Beaconsfield had rather a restless night till three A.M. Since then his Lordship has had some quiet sleep. Cough and expectoration less troublesome, and his strength maintained."

The doctors expressed themselves fairly satisfied with the condition of their patient, but the continuance of the keen north-east winds caused them much anxiety. Dr. Bruce remained at the house during the day, and both of the other physicians in attendance called two or three times; but it was not considered necessary to issue another bulletin until night. Considerable anxiety was shown by the numerous callers, amongst whom were the Duke of Cambridge and Sir Stafford Northcote, both of whom had personal interviews with Lord Barrington. The verbal reports given out from time to time were, however, of a nature to quell alarm, as Lord Beaconsfield was able to sleep well at intervals and take nourishment freely, while there was no return of spasm.

Dr. Quain arrived at the house at nine o'clock in the evening, and was with Lord Beaconsfield about an hour, after which the physicians held their ordinary consultation. While this was progressing the Prince of Wales and the Duke of Edinburgh, who had just arrived from St. Petersburg, drove up to the house, and had an interview with the doctors, together with Lord Barrington and Sir Philip Rose, of nearly half an hour's duration. After their Royal Highnesses had left a bulletin to the following effect was communicated:—"Lord Beaconsfield has passed a quiet day, free from spasmodic breathing. To-night there is a slight increase of fever, indicated by the state of the pulse and temperature."

The enormous sympathy manifested in Lord Beaconsfield's state was shown, not only by the innumerable calls in Curzon Street, but by the telegrams constantly received from all parts of the world, and by offers, many of them of a very singular kind, of objects for the comfort or the cure of the distinguished invalid.

April 5. The bulletin of Tuesday morning, April 5, was calculated to allay some of the alarm which the accounts of the previous day had excited. Dr. Quain arrived at Curzon Street at half-past nine, and the result of the consultation with Dr. Kidd and Dr. Bruce, both of whom had been at the house throughout the night, declared itself as follows:—"Lord Beaconsfield has passed a tolerably quiet night. Some fresh gout has appeared in the knees, which will explain the occurrence of feverish symptoms which were present last night, and which are mitigated this morning. His Lordship continues to take nourishment and his strength is maintained." Personal inquiries elicited the additional information that Lord Beaconsfield was very cheerful, and appeared to take more interest in public affairs than for some days past. His request that he should see the morning bulletin issued by his physician was complied with. Dr. Kidd called again about half-past one and saw his patient, who he stated to be progressing as well as could be expected. Later, however, there was a return of the spasms, followed by a speedy rally, without much apparent loss of strength. Between three and four o'clock a letter was received from the Queen, which was read to the distinguished invalid by Lord Barrington, who then saw his Lordship for the first time since his relapse two days previously.

The physicians were again in attendance at nine o'clock, and this was their report:—" Lord Beaconsfield had a return of spasms in the early part of the afternoon. This attack was slighter than those of the preceding days, and has been followed by a less amount of prostration. The chest symptoms are not worse. His Lordship has taken nourishment well during the afternoon." It was in the course of this day, April 5, that Lord Barrington received a telegram from Lord Rowton to the effect that he had arrived at Monte Carlo with his sister, and would leave again for England immediately.

Throughout Tuesday night the improvement in the condition of Lord Beaconsfield continued. While the gout and chest symptoms generally improved, there was an almost entire cessation of the spasmodic attacks that had chiefly caused anxiety, and his Lordship was able to take nourishment with less difficulty, whilst he slept at intervals. Both Dr. Bruce and Dr. Kidd remained at Curzon Street on Tuesday night, the former retiring to rest while his colleague remained

April 6.

on duty. They were, as usual, joined at half-past nine the next morning by Dr. Quain, the result of the consultation being the publication of a bulletin to the following effect:—" Lord Beaconsfield has passed a fair night. The symptoms generally as regards the chest and the gout are improved. His Lordship's condition is, on the whole, favourable." This report was received with great satisfaction by those waiting for it, and was immediately telegraphed to her Majesty by Lord Barrington, who also sent copies by messengers to the Prince of Wales, the Duke of Edinburgh, Mr. Gladstone, and other distinguished personages. To prevent the incessant opening and closing of the front door, two copies of the bulletin were placed on boards suspended to the railings outside the house. The beneficial effect of this arrangement was amply shown in the course of the day by the increased quiet inside the building.

Dr. Kidd returned to Curzon Street at about one o'clock, and saw Lord Beaconsfield for a short time. On leaving, he stated that his patient had passed a good morning, and was doing well. At a second visit shortly before five he was met by Dr. Quain. No regular consultation took place, and no bulletin was issued, but the fact that the physicians were satisfied with the progress that Lord Beaconsfield was making was telegraphed to her Majesty at Osborne. The Prince of Wales called at a little

after seven o'clock, and had a short interview with Dr. Bruce. At nine o'clock the three physicians held a consultation, of which this was the result:—
"During the day Lord Beaconsfield has been almost entirely free from spasms. He has taken nourishment with less difficulty. The symptoms generally show improvement."

A change for the worse, however, declared itself during Wednesday night, and at three o'clock on Thursday morning, April 7, Lord Beaconsfield was seized with severe spasms, accompanied by slight congestion of the right lung. Dr. Quain was immediately sent for by Drs. Kidd and Bruce, and reached Curzon Street at a little before four o'clock. Soon after his arrival Sir William Jenner called to see Dr. Quain, and remained some considerable time. Dr. Jenner was understood thoroughly to approve the treatment applied. Messengers were also despatched for Lord Barrington and Sir Philip Rose, both of whom arrived within a few minutes. They were joined at seven o'clock by Lord Rowton, who had just reached England from the Continent. Dr. Quain did not leave the house until half-past eight, and returned at ten o'clock, when the physicians held their usual morning consultation. At a quarter to eleven the public read this statement as follows:—"During the night Lord Beaconsfield had a severe attack of difficulty of breathing, with some congestion of the right lung, brought on by a slight chill. The

<small>April 7.</small>

symptoms, which at the time created grave anxiety, have nearly passed away, leaving his Lordship not materially worse than prior to the attack."

Drs. Quain and Kidd left Curzon Street at about half-past eleven, when they stated that Lord Beaconsfield was quiet and comfortable, and, although slightly weaker, not seriously the worse for the severe attack in the night. The physicians again paid a short visit at a little before four, when they found their patient maintaining his condition of the morning; it was therefore considered unnecessary to issue any extra bulletin. At nine o'clock when they returned they issued the following:—" Lord Beaconsfield has passed the day free from any distressing symptoms. His Lordship's weakness—incident to the course of his malady—is now a chief source of anxiety." Personal inquiries elicited the additional information that there was very little change since the morning, and that his Lordship was as well as could be expected.

April 8.  Dr. Kidd and Dr. Bruce again remained during Thursday night at Curzon Street, and on Friday morning Dr. Quain joined his colleagues shortly after half-past nine, the following bulletin being issued shortly afterwards:—" Lord Beaconsfield has passed a good night; had refreshing sleep; taken nourishment well. The symptoms caused by the serious relapse of the previous night are passing away. His Lordship's condition this morning is more hopeful than it was yesterday." Dr. Quain paid his second visit of the day between four and five o'clock. On leaving, he stated that his patient had not lost ground, and that the favourable symptoms developed in the morning were fully maintained. The physicians returned, as usual, at nine o'clock, and held their evening consultation, when their bulletin was as follows :—" Lord Beaconsfield has passed the day without material change, the favourable condition of the morning being maintained."

April 9. The physicians met on Saturday morning at half-past nine, and at eleven o'clock issued the following bulletin :—"Lord Beaconsfield's night has been somewhat restless. He has been rather less inclined to take nourishment. His Lordship's condition, however, is not materially different from that of yesterday." Dr. Quain and Dr. Kidd both paid visits during the day to their patient, whom they reported to be going on as well as they could expect, and again met at night, after which they issued the following :—" Lord Beaconsfield has passed the day freer from any of the symptoms of his chest affection or of gout; but his Lordship has felt, and is, weak."

April 10. As on previous nights, Drs. Bruce and Kidd stayed at Curzon Street, and were joined in the morning by Dr. Quain. This was the bulletin :—"Lord Beaconsfield has passed a very quiet night, and has taken nourishment well, but the weakness continues much the same." Dr. Quain paid his last visit

for the day at nine o'clock, and the bulletin said:—
"Lord Beaconsfield passed the day favourably, rather
gaining than losing strength, until 8.0 P.M., when
he had an attack of spasmodic breathing, which was
relieved by expectoration. His Lordship's condition
is not materially affected by this attack."

April 11.   Dr. Quain arrived at half-past nine on Monday, and
at eleven o'clock the following was issued:—"Lord
Beaconsfield has passed a somewhat restless night.
His chest symptoms are not worse, but his Lordship's
strength is somewhat diminished."

During the morning Lord Beaconsfield saw Lord
Rowton, for the first time since his return from
Algiers. Dr. Quain and Dr. Kidd called twice in the
course of the afternoon, and after their second visit
they reported that Lord Beaconsfield had passed a
quiet day, and had rather gained than lost strength.
Between five and six o'clock the Prince and Princess
of Wales, the latter of whom had only just arrived
at Charing Cross from St. Petersburg, drove direct
to Curzon Street to make inquiries as to the condition of Lord Beaconsfield. Their Royal Highnesses
remained in conversation with Lord Rowton for
about twenty minutes. Shortly after nine o'clock
Drs. Quain and Kidd returned, and a few minutes
later Sir William Jenner, by special command of the
Queen, arrived, and joined in the consultation with
the other physicians, the result of which was the
issue of a bulletin to the following effect:—"Lord

Beaconsfield has passed the day favourably, taken more ·nourishment, and to some extent regained strength." After the consultation Sir William Jenner and Dr. Quain left.

The result of the consultation of the next day may be judged from the following:—" Lord Beaconsfield has passed a tolerably fair night. His Lordship has been free from distressing symptoms, and the gain of strength acquired during the afternoon of yesterday has been maintained." After Drs. Quain and Kidd had left, Lord Beaconsfield took some refreshment, and at mid-day was considered to be sufficiently strong to be removed into the next room. This was done under the superintendence of Dr. Bruce. All through the morning, as during the previous two or three days, a great many working men gathered in Curzon Street and anxiously inquired for the latest information. This fact was reported to Lord Beaconsfield by Lord Rowton.

April 12.

Dr. Kidd returned to the house about four o'clock, and Dr. Quain about three-quarters of an hour later. The latter left after a short visit, when he stated that Lord Beaconsfield had been rather more restless, and appeared somewhat weaker than in the morning, but that otherwise there was no material change. At seven o'clock Dr. Quain was again hastily summoned, as his patient had been seized with a severe attack of difficulty in breathing. The usual remedies were at once administered, and, after a time, the trouble passed off, Lord Beaconsfield being again able to take some slight nourishment. At nine o'clock the physicians met again for consultation, and an hour afterwards the following bulletin was published :—" Lord Beaconsfield has passed rather a restless day. At seven o'clock this evening he had a severe attack of difficulty of breathing, but this has passed off, and his Lordship is now sleeping quietly, having taken some nourishment." The physicians supplemented the bulletin with the statement that each recurring attack of the spasmodic breathing necessarily rendered their patient weaker and the chances of recovery more remote, and that while they did not despair, they could not disguise the fact that Lord Beaconsfield's condition was precarious.

The next day a slight improvement was reported in the condition of Lord Beaconsfield. Dr. Quain arrived for the morning consultation at half-past nine, and the following was the bulletin :—" Lord Beaconsfield has passed another restless night, and felt disinclined to take nourishment. His Lordship is less weak this morning than might have been expected under the circumstances." In the afternoon the physicians met at the house, when it was resolved to issue a supplementary bulletin to allay public anxiety. Shortly before six o'clock the following was posted outside the house :—" Lord Beaconsfield has passed a quiet day, free from any material discomfort. He has taken nourishment and had rest. The strength is somewhat greater." Sir William Jenner paid a short visit to Lord Beaconsfield during the evening, and at nine o'clock the three physicians published the following :—" Lord Beaconsfield passed the day without the occurrence of any symptom to create anxiety or alarm. He has taken a moderate amount of nutritious food with less repugnance. There is rather an increase of strength since the last bulletin."

The weather had now become comparatively mild, and the change apparently had the desired effect upon Lord Beaconsfield, who seemed much stronger and very cheerful. This improvement was aided by wheeling the bed of the invalid from the front to the back drawing-room, both large and airy apartments, upon alternate days. The chest symptoms were presumed to have almost disappeared, but the great debility of the patient necessitated the most watchful attention and care.

The usual consultation was held on Thursday morning, April 14, at ten o'clock, and the bulletin said:— "Lord Beaconsfield has passed a good night. The chest symptoms are quiet. There is some gain in the digestive power and in the strength." *April 14.*

The extreme anxiety of the Queen as to the condition of Lord Beaconsfield continued to be shown in frequent telegrams and messages, and her Majesty expressed her gratification at the general interest shown by the country at large in the welfare of the distinguished statesman. The Prince of Wales and the Duke of Cambridge called at Curzon Street between one and two o'clock on Tuesday afternoon, and had an interview of nearly half an hour with Lords Rowton and Barrington. In the course of the day Lord Beaconsfield was visited by both Drs. Quain and Kidd, who stated in reply to inquiries that their patient was progressing as well as they could hope, but no further bulletin was issued until after the evening consultation, when the following appeared:—" Lord Beaconsfield has passed the day favourably. He has taken nourishment, has had quiet sleep, and regained strength in some degree."

Lord Beaconsfield's sick-room in Curzon Street had now become the centre of a professional controversy, an adequate idea of which may be formed from the following remarks in a leading article in *The Standard* of April 15 :—" The statements which have recently been made public by the medical advisers of Lord Beaconsfield will be scanned with legitimate curiosity, not unmingled with some feeling of impatience. Lord Beaconsfield has for some years past been attended by Dr. Kidd, a duly qualified member of the profession, but inclined to the particular style of treatment known as homœopathy. This system has been condemned by the English faculty as heretical, and those who adhere to it are exposed to a kind of professional excommunication, according to which no regular practitioner is allowed to co-operate with them in the management of a case. Such being the known rules to which all orthodox physicians are expected to conform, it became a question of some difficulty, when it was thought desirable that Lord Beaconsfield should have further advice, to whom his friends were to apply. Agreeably to the noble Lord's own wishes, an application was made to Dr. Quain, who replied in the first instance that he did not see how it was possible for him to consult with Dr. Kidd, as the latter was a homœopathist.

"On this he was informed by Lord Barrington that, at all events, Lord Beaconsfield had not been treated homœopathically, but in accordance with the ordinary principles applicable to his complaint. Dr. Quain then required that Dr. Kidd himself should make a statement to this effect in writing; and this request being granted, and Dr. Quain having taken the opinion of some of the leading members of the profession, considered himself at liberty to act in concert with Dr. Kidd. Dr. Quain has been greatly blamed by some members of the faculty for having consented to meet Dr. Kidd under any circumstances; but we feel assured that had he refused to see Lord Beaconsfield he would have exposed not only himself, but the whole profession, to the severest censure.

"It would be monstrous, therefore, to find any

fault with Dr. Quain for having consented to act with Dr. Kidd. He seems to us to have behaved in a perfectly straightforward and honourable manner. Fully alive to the dignity of his profession, and by no means underrating the value of the rules which have been adopted for the protection of scientific orthodoxy, he deemed it his duty to make certain inquiries with regard to Dr. Kidd's system before he felt justified in acting with him; but on receiving an assurance from Dr. Kidd that, although he certainly believed in the efficacy of homœopathic treatment in certain cases, he was not a regular homœopathist, and that only the ordinary remedies recognised by the profession at large had been applied to his distinguished patient, he was ready at once to give him the benefit of his assistance. In this view of the case he was confirmed by the opinion of the then President of the College of Physicians and other eminent practitioners; nor do we see what more can be required of him in the way of explanation or excuse.

"As much, however, can hardly be said for the conduct of Sir William Jenner. Sir William was applied to in the first instance by Dr. Kidd himself to consult with him on the condition of Lord Beaconsfield. This Sir William Jenner at once declined to do, on the ground that Dr. Kidd was a homœopathist, and without asking any questions which would have enabled Lord Beaconsfield's physician to explain to what extent he really deserved that designation. Sir William, it seems, was afterwards induced to visit Lord Beaconsfield by the 'commands of the Queen,' having previously refused to do so, because such an act would have been a violation of those rules which he deemed essential to the welfare of his profession.

"Now, without entering upon the very delicate question how far even the entreaty of the Sovereign should overrule a man's regard for the highest interests of his profession, we unhesitatingly assert that when Sir William Jenner was informed of the resolution taken by Dr. Quain, he was bound to consider whether that eminent physician might not have had good reason for adopting it. He had no right to assume without inquiry that Dr. Quain was wrong, and when we now see under what very high authority Dr. Quain was acting, it is more than doubtful whether Sir William Jenner will not find himself in a false position. Rules such as those by which he supposed himself to be bound defeat their own object when applied with such excessive stringency.

"Moreover, we are at a loss to understand what middle course could possibly be found between the course adopted by Sir William and that adopted by Dr. Quain. If the allopathist is to hold himself absolutely aloof under all conceivable circumstances from those who differ from him, patients must very often be deprived of that assistance which might possibly save their lives. If he is not to do this, and is to hold that under especial pressure he is justified in departing somewhat from the strict letter of the law, it is difficult to see how he could act with more propriety than Dr. Quain has done. For Dr. Quain to have made no inquiry at all, and to have driven straight down to Curzon Street as soon as the application was made to him, would have been to run into the opposite extreme, and Sir William Jenner and his friends cannot surely mean to imply that this would have been the proper course of action. The public may possibly be of opinion that even Dr. Quain himself was a little over-sensitive on the point, and that valuable lives ought not to be trifled with in deference to scruples on a matter of professional etiquette. But be this as it may, we think very few persons outside the medical profession will on the present occasion approve the conduct of Sir William Jenner."

These observations elicited the following reply the next day from Sir W. Gull :—

To the Editor of "The Standard."

Sir,—As, in *The Standard* of to-day, you express, as from a public point of view, some censure on Sir William Jenner for not complying with Dr. Kidd's request to meet him in consultation, will you afford me space to say that I desire to bear my part in that censure, whatever it may be?

Sir William Jenner, as a friend and colleague, conferred with me before answering Dr. Kidd's note, and I entirely concurred with him in his reply, which was to the effect that, though ready to give his services in so anxious and important a case, he could not, consistently with his duty to the patient, co-operate with one who, according to his own statement, has a double set of convictions in the treatment of disease. For, whatever other objections might be raised as to etiquette and the like, it is certain that the welfare of a patient is endangered when there is a tendency to compromise.

I am, Sir, your obedient servant,

WILLIAM W. GULL.

*74, Brook Street, April 15.*

April

The weather still remained mild, and Lord Beaconsfield as a consequence continued to improve. On Good Friday the bulletin issued by the physicians after the morning consultation at ten o'clock, was to the following effect:—"The only change to report in Lord Beaconsfield's condition this morning is one of slowly progressive improvement." It was further stated that this bulletin was to be considered as entirely comprehensive, and covering the fact that there had not only been no recurrence of the spasmodic attacks, but that the chest symptoms and gout had apparently given way to treatment. Dr. Quain paid a passing visit at about four o'clock, but, in consequence of the excellent report given him, did not see his patient. Both he and Dr. Kidd returned at nine o'clock, and a little later this bulletin was posted:—" Lord Beaconsfield has passed a quiet day, free from discomfort, and maintained the gain of strength already acquired."

The report of the physicians on Saturday morning was not unfavourable:—"Lord Beaconsfield was restless during part of last night; but this morning his Lordship's condition is satisfactory, and his progress though slow, is not interrupted." It appeared that the restlessness only lasted an hour, after which Lord Beaconsfield again slept soundly and on waking was able to take some nourishment. Prince Leopold called at Curzon Street about one o'clock and had an interview of a quarter of an hour's duration with Lords Rowton and Barrington. In the afternoon Lord Beaconsfield was sufficiently strong to see both Lord Barrington and Sir Philip Rose, the latter of whom was much astonished at the progress made by the noble Earl, who conversed freely and cheerfully with his visitors.

Dr. Quain arrived in the evening, at a little after nine. The consultation which followed resulted in the issue of the following:—" Lord Beaconsfield has passed the day favourably." Dr. Quain and Dr. Kidd, the latter of whom had been in attendance at Curzon Street for the previous twenty nights, then left, Dr. Mitchell Bruce remaining with the patient. Both physicians returned at ten on Sunday morning, when they issued another bulletin, confirmatory of the early morning report that his Lordship had passed a comfortable night, and was going on as well as could be expected:—" Lord Beaconsfield has had several hours' sleep during the night, and taken the requisite nourishment. This morning his Lordship's condition remains very much as yesterday."

In the evening Dr. Quain arrived at Curzon Street soon after nine, and remained in consultation with Drs. Kidd and Bruce for about half-an-hour. The bulletin declared :—" Lord Beaconsfield has passed the day without any material change. There has been no marked progress during the day and no unfavourable change." Lord Beaconsfield during the afternoon conversed with Lord Barrington for some time.

In the course of Easter Sunday the wind had again gone round to the north-east. It became bitterly cold at night, and the effects of the change were shown in the bulletin issued on Monday :—" During the last twenty-four hours it may be said that, on the whole, as compared with the preceding twenty-four hours, Lord Beaconsfield has been rather more restless, and taken rather less nourishment ; as a consequence, there has been no material gain of strength." After the consultation, Dr. Quain intimated that although there had been no gain of strength within the past twenty-four hours, there had been no loss of vital power. Lord Rowton stayed in Curzon Street during the whole of the afternoon, and saw his lordship—who was able to talk—several times. But the evening bulletin was alarmingly unfavourable :—" Lord Beaconsfield's condition has not been satisfactory during the day. He

*April 1*

has been free from urgent symptoms, and taken more nourishment; yet he rather loses strength." After the consultation, Dr. Quain, on leaving, said his patient was very weak and low.

pril 19.   This last bulletin was received with grave apprehension. It was generally regarded as an indication that the life of Lord Beaconsfield was fast ebbing away; though it was hardly thought that the end was so near as it proved to be. As midnight approached, the drowsiness that had been apparent gradually deepened into stupor, this in turn being superseded by almost complete insensibility. About three o'clock the breathing became embarrassed, and for the first time the restoratives applied by the physicians did not have their usual effect. Dr. Quain was immediately summoned, but all efforts to maintain life were in vain. At half-past six on Tuesday morning, April 19, the following notice was written by Lord Barrington on black-edged paper, and posted outside the house on the bulletin board, where it was eagerly scanned throughout the day by the large and sympathetic crowds who flocked to the vicinity of the darkened house: —" The debility, which was evidently increasing yesterday, progressed during the night, and Lord Beaconsfield died at half-past four this morning, calmly, as if in sleep."

By the bed-side of Lord Beaconsfield at the time of his death were Lords Rowton and Barrington and

Sir Philip Rose, together with his physicians and the faithful attendants who have for weeks past stayed by him night and day. Doctors Kidd and Bruce, together with Lord Rowton, had been with Lord Beaconsfield throughout the night; but the other gentlemen, together with Mr. Ralph Disraeli, were sent for shortly after three o'clock, when it was perceived that a great change had taken place, and that the critical period was at hand. Mr. Disraeli was, unfortunately, unable to reach Curzon Street in time to be with his brother at the last.

The actual complaint to which Lord Beaconsfield succumbed was an attack of acute bronchitis supervening on chronic disease, complicated by age and gout in the system—a system greatly exhausted by incessant and devoted attention to public business. Beyond this, both the brain and heart appeared to have been healthy. For the last three years the departed statesman had been suffering from the disease, with periodically severer attacks. His final illness, it will be seen, lasted nearly a month, and threatened at the close of the first week to prove fatal. The weather was during the greater portion of the time of the most unpropitious character, a bitter east wind penetrating everywhere, notwithstanding the utmost precautions that could be taken. With its cessation on the 15th of April, Lord Beaconsfield's symptoms somewhat improved; with its return on Saturday there came a further relapse. Lord

Beaconsfield became more restless, took nourishment with more irregularity and less willingness, and gradually grew worse, till at last, without any struggle, he expired, so gently that it was some few moments after death before those watching around his couch were aware of the fact.

One of Lord Beaconsfield's medical attendants furnished the following particulars of the Earl's last moments:—The Earl's drowsiness, which had been apparent in the later part of the night of April 18, gradually deepened towards midnight into a stupor, from which his Lordship was with difficulty aroused. He still, however, took nourishment up to half-past one the next morning. About two o'clock the stupor deepened into coma, or complete insensibility, and towards the hour of three the breathing became very much embarrassed. Dr. Kidd and Dr. Bruce at once applied all the usual restoratives for the breathing, but for the first time during his illness there was no response. Seeing the approach of death, Dr. Kidd immediately despatched messengers to Lord Barrington, Sir Philip Rose, and Sir William Jenner. Lord Barrington was the first to arrive, and upon entering the sick room he found Lord Rowton closely grasping the right hand of the distinguished patient, in which grasp Lord Barrington joined. The two noble lords continued to clasp the right hand of Lord Beaconsfield until the last moment, his left being all the time held in that of

Dr. Kidd. About five minutes before the breathing ceased Sir Philip Rose and Dr. Quain arrived. Then a most placid appearance came over his Lordship's face, which deeply moved all in the room. The distressing breathing ceased, and for about five minutes, slow, gentle inspiration took its place, and all seemed over; but even after the breathing had stopped for four or five minutes, the heart's action kept up, and the pulse continued perfectly perceptible at the wrist. It was a most touching scene. As Lord Rowton, Lord Barrington, the three physicians, Mr. Baum, the young servant James, and the two nurses watched round the bed for a further period of ten minutes, perfect silence was kept, save for the weeping of some who were present, because even when the pulse ceased it was difficult to realise that he was dead. Thus, without suffering, without a struggle, Lord Beaconsfield's life slowly passed away.

During the progress of his illness Lord Beaconsfield displayed his usual fortitude. He was patient and reticent, speaking but little, as he found that the exertion of doing so fatigued him. When, however, he did converse, his remarks always showed his characteristic shrewdness, and it was evident to those with him that when silent he was often absorbed in a deep train of thought. He was never better for interviews with friends or others, and consequently did not encourage them—a course in which he was sustained by the advice of his physicians.

Indeed, he hesitated for some two or three days to see Lord Rowton after his return from Algiers, fearing the excitement might be injurious; but after the first interview the latter was constantly with him, and Lord Beaconsfield derived the greatest possible comfort from his presence. With this exception, and on one or two occasions when Lord Barrington and Sir Philip Rose saw him, no one but his medical advisers and personal attendants were admitted to the sick-room.

Immediately after all was over, telegrams were sent to her Majesty, the Prince of Wales, the Duke of Edinburgh, and other members of the Royal Family, as well as to Mr. Gladstone at Hawarden, the noble Earl's colleagues, and to the Representatives of the various Foreign Powers.

Telegrams of condolence were received in reply from all parts of the globe. Amongst them was one of sympathy from Mr. Gladstone, who was deeply affected when he received the sad intelligence of Lord Beaconsfield's death.

The Prince of Wales sent a special messenger during the afternoon from Sandringham with letters of condolence to Lord Rowton and Lord Barrington.

Dean Stanley called at a little before noon, and saw Lord Rowton and Mr. Ralph Disraeli. The Dean made an offer of a resting-place in the Abbey for the noble Earl, but no answer could be given at the time, as, although Lord Beaconsfield had made no allusion during his last illness as to where he wished to be buried, he had frequently on previous occasions expressed his desire to be placed by the side of Viscountess Beaconsfield at Hughenden. In the afternoon Sir Philip Rose went down to Hughenden Manor in company with Lord Rowton, the literary trustee under the provisions of the will, to look through the private papers of his Lordship, and ascertain if he had left any written instructions on the subject.

The *Court Newsman* of April 19 contained the following significant paragraph:—" The Queen received this morning, with feelings of deepest sorrow, the sad intelligence of the death of the Earl of Beaconsfield, in whom her Majesty loses a most valued and devoted friend and counsellor, and the nation one of its most distinguished statesmen."

## III.

### IMPRESSIONS PRODUCED BY DEATH.

Some idea of the impressions which Lord Beaconsfield's death produced on the Continent may be formed from the following extracts from the chief journals of France, Germany, Austria, and Italy. The French press delivered itself to the following effect:—

"Lord Beaconsfield (said the *Français*) died at five this morning. The son of Isaac Disraeli ends his existence environed with all the honours and all the regrets that England can bestow upon a subject of the Queen. The noble Lord has, in his seventy-seventh year, brought to a close one of the most extraordinary and most active of careers. History no doubt will not invariably approve all the acts done throughout his life by this dauntless champion, who conquered the first rank by dint of sheer strength of will and talent; but it can never contest the great services he rendered his country and the Party which chose him as its chief. The embarrassment in which his death will leave the Opposition, the sincere regret of his adversaries now in office, the general mourning at his loss, in which the Queen herself takes a leading part, alike testify to the great position Lord Beaconsfield held in the institutions of his country, and to the great void caused by his departure from this world."

This is from the *Debats*:—

"Many conflicting judgments will no doubt be passed upon the statesman and the *littérateur*, but no one will venture to contest his mighty originality, his brilliant qualities as a writer, and his incomparable qualities as an orator; none will ever deny him the glory of having been, whether in Opposition or in office, the most trusted representative, the staunchest champion of that non-exclusive Toryism which has known how to modify and transform itself daily, and which has enabled the aristocracy of England to remain Liberal without ceasing to be Conservative."

The *République Française*, the organ of M. Gambetta, said:—

"England has just lost one of the most brilliant individualities that during this century has impassioned Party struggles in the British Empire. Lord Beaconsfield's death will create no surprise, but it will excite throughout England that boundless sorrow felt by all parties without distinction when a Statesman who for close upon half a century has played a preponderating part in the affairs of his country disappears from the political arena. People reflect, and not without reason, that so highly gifted a champion cannot so long have retained his popularity among a free people without having contributed to the greatness of his country, and few men are called upon to the same extent as Lord Beaconsfield to reap the benefit of that kind of amnesty which death grants to those whose career is marked only by sincere errors or shortcomings. If he made mistakes, the British nation is partly responsible for them; if he often erred, England participated in his error, and did so all the more passionately that Lord Beaconsfield, with his adventurous tendencies and that thirsting for the marvellous which was, so to speak, the trade mark of his mind, exercised over his compatriots a seduction all the more extraordinary that it did not chime in with the temperament of the mass of the nation. The Leader of the Tory Party was nearly seventy-seven, but never had his personality shone with greater splendour than at the period which is generally regarded as the decline of life. In the eyes of the nation Lord Beaconsfield was still young, for up to the very last his words and acts were singularly free from any indication of fatigue or senility. Neither he nor his policy was aged, and that is not one of the least marvellous features of a career in which the marvellous has been so conspicuous. It is quite possible to disapprove of the ideas and principles of which

Lord Beaconsfield made himself the zealous champion for forty years, and to deplore the adventures into which he was hurried by his enterprising genius; but it would be an insult to the people who accepted, applauded, and acclaimed him to withhold a kind of admiration. A number of misdeeds have been laid to his charge; he has been reproached with being deficient in depth, in *coup d'œil*, and even in moral courage. If he had really had all these defects, we think that the public feeling would speedily have turned against him. The Tory Leader will not rank as one of the great arbiters of the destinies of mankind, but his career will endure as a proof of what may be achieved by a skilful mind complying with admirable suppleness with the transformations of public opinion. What energy and perseverance Mr. Disraeli must have needed from the day when, hooted by the Whig majority in Parliament, he retorted that the day would come when they would hear him, to the time when the great Conservative Party chose him as its leader, and he forced himself upon his country! Without inheriting a fortune—in a country where wealth and birth used to be the indispensable passports to public life—he was able to overcome obstacles believed to be insurmountable, and to conquer by the sheer force of his own indomitable will the position which everything conspired to prevent his obtaining. It was a great revenge of Israel over Christendom. Once having attained a foremost rank in the Conservative Party, he was able to make it amenable to that discipline that has been one of the reasons for its successes, and make it accept that policy of conciliation and compromise with popular aspirations, one of the most memorable results of which was the passing of the Reform Bill by a Tory Administration. At bottom Lord Beaconsfield appears to us to have been a clear-sighted sceptic. He had with remarkable precision calculated the advantage which, from a Governmental point of view, he could derive from the position of the Conservative Party. No one foresaw more clearly than he did the future in store for it. He knew quite well there was no stopping the Liberal evolution slowly being accomplished in England. Instead of waging open war with Liberalism, he compounded with it, and, by dint of concessions, cleverly made at the right time, he contrived to grant only a portion of what public opinion demanded. The whole Conservatism of Lord Beaconsfield consisted in retarding the English political evolution whilst very closely following it. By a series of combinations skilfully combined he saved the Party he directed from unpopularity and discredit. In this respect he did the Tories a service, the value of which it is impossible to exaggerate. Lord Beaconsfield, if not a great politician, was at all events a great tactician. That may not be enough to control the destinies of a powerful nation, but it is more than is required to preserve a Party from premature dissolution. The death of Lord Beaconsfield will therefore cause a great void in the ranks of the Tories. These latter were in the highest degree subject to the influence of the illustrious deceased. Deprived of the chief who had brought them safely through so many difficulties, who had made acceptable to them compromises which their caste prejudice would have rejected, it is a question whether the Party will be able to keep up the intelligent discipline to which Lord Beaconsfield had trained them. The Conservative Party never had greater need of it. The principle of large landed estates is daily attacked in England with increasing vigour, and its defence is becoming more and more arduous. The British aristocracy contains enough brilliant and cultivated minds to carry on the struggle with *éclat*, but it loses its chief at the very time when his assistance was most needful. Lord Beaconsfield's successor has not yet revealed himself, and whatever his capacities may be, he cannot possess that popular ascendency which Lord Beaconsfield derived from his *quasi* plebeian origin and the *prestige* that attaches to those who owe everything to their own talent."

The Radical *Mot d'Ordre* wrote:

"The habit we have taken in France to regard Mr. Gladstone as the impersonation of Liberalism, and to identify Conservatism with his illustrious rival, is founded on error. In reality there is no practical difference in their political theories between the present Premier, imbued from his tenderest youth with Protestant bigotry, and his rival, who brought his broad and intelligent scepticism to bear on all questions. We French Radicals would be greatly puzzled to choose between them. But what preference we have is in favour of Benjamin Disraeli. His tendencies were more democratic than those of his rival. He never at any time interfered in any way with the freedom of the press and the right of meeting, which he justly described in 1865 as 'the two safety-valves of a great country.' The Reform Bill which he carried in 1867 was infinitely more liberal than that introduced by Mr. Gladstone in the preceding year. Had he been in office in 1870, we should in all probability not have been crushed by Prussia; and we cannot forget that to his intervention far more than that of Russia we are indebted for having been spared another war with Prussia in 1875. At the General Election of 1874, when for the first time in the Parliamentary annals of Great Britain two working men took their seats in the House of Commons, Benjamin Disraeli, then virtually Premier, had the happy inspiration of hailing as a beneficial sign of the times this accession of the labouring classes to public life, and welcoming Mr. Burt and Mr. Macdonald in terms which none of our French Radicals would think of using."

The *Soleil* said :—

"Notwithstanding his defeat, just one year ago,

Lord Beaconsfield continued very popular on the other side of the Channel. The English felt grateful to him for having restored to their flag on several points of the globe a *prestige* that had been sadly impaired. In his turn Mr. Gladstone had been losing ground since his accession to office, and it is impossible to say what might not have been the result of the next General Election if death had not deprived the Conservative Party of its redoubtable Chief. All that was done by Lord Beaconsfield in the course of his long and brilliant career is not equally entitled to praise, but no one can question the intellect and energy of this exceptional man. He rendered services to his country which even his enemies acknowledge, and in an age in which Positivism and Materialism tend to bring down all things to their low level, he was able to rescue England from the grovelling *terre-à-terre* of the Manchester school, raise up her soul, and remind her that mere petty ephemeral interests are not everything for a great people. Amid the fogs of England Lord Beaconsfield shone out as a bright luminary. His death produces the effect of an eclipse."

The following is from the *Siècle :—*

" This bereavement will be keenly felt in England, where, since the illness of the Prince of Wales, no such manifestation of sympathy has been witnessed as during the malady of Lord Beaconsfield. Not only has the Conservative Party been deprived of its Leader, but England has also lost a man who was at the same time an eminent writer and a remarkable statesman. Lord Beaconsfield has made for himself a place in the glorious annals of English Prime Ministers, and we cannot forget that of them all he was the one the least subject to the national prejudices against France."

The *Parlement* remarked :—

"In office he displayed the same qualities as in Opposition. His policy was bold, supple, subtle, and rich in expedients. Without firing a cannon-shot he succeeded in acquiring Cyprus and in depriving Russia of the most precious of the results obtained during the late war. England, who had witnessed with folded arms the dismemberment of Denmark, the incorporation of Hanover into Prussia, and the denunciation of the Treaty of Paris by Russia, at length resumed a leading part in the destinies of Europe, and occupied in the Congress of Berlin a place worthy of her historical antecedents."

The *Clairon* observed :—

"The greatest member of the Conservative Party has vanished from the stage, and France has lost its most illustrious and avowed friend amongst British Statesmen. The figure which has disappeared was grand and original, and we desire to salute in him above all the personification of our political tendencies and our patriotic instincts. As

Premier, he showed Europe that England was something more than a counting-house. He obtained partial possession of the Suez Canal by the purchase of shares to the amount of four millions. He established that preponderance against which we have protested in these very columns. He placed the Imperial crown of India on his Sovereign's head. He made Russia halt at the very doors of Constantinople. He took possession of Cyprus, and caused the weight of the British arms to be felt in every continent, struggling at one and the same time against savages, civilised nations, and his eternal enemy, Mr. Gladstone, who sought to make England disgusted with glory in order to cast it back into egotism."

The *Moniteur Universel* said:—

"With Lord Beaconsfield disappears a figure,—we should rather say a political force,—which had its place and played its part in the equilibrium of Western Europe. He dominated his contemporaries by strength of character, talent, and vigour. He could hold his own with the most distinguished men, and oblige them to count with him. Now that Lord Beaconsfield has disappeared, there remain in Europe none but improvised and ephemeral Ministers, reeds bending before every wind, puny and inexperienced politicians, the scene being occupied by one personage alone, Prince Bismarck. We seek in vain for something to cast an obstacle in the way of German hegemony, for something to weaken and oppose its expansion in Europe and Asia. The Imperial Chancellor is left free to act as he likes. The Continent is his."

Among Berlin papers the *Tribune*, the organ representing the Left wing of the National Liberals, wrote as follows :—

"From his first appearance in the literary and political world Benjamin Disraeli commanded an ever-increasing share of public attention. Universally rated a wonderful man when he was a mere youth, he enjoyed the same enviable reputation up to the day of his death as a septuagenarian. However varied the character of the epoch in which he was called upon to act, however serious the nature of the events in which it was his lot to play a part, Benjamin Disraeli always knew how to elicit the interest, charm the imagination, and command the respect of the world. In him there was a combination of qualities any one of which would have sufficed to raise him high above the ordinary level of mankind. Though the writings of Isaac Disraeli are still accounted eminent contributions towards English literature, the first lines Benjamin published gave promise of a talent vastly superior to that of his father. While his imagination and poetry allured young and old, his political wisdom and enthusiasm riveted old and young. We all remember the famous sentence he flung at the heads of adverse members, who treated him as a *parvenu*, and declined to listen to his first speech in the House. He fully kept the promise he then gave, and will ever be regarded as the regenerator of the Tory Party at a time when regeneration was direly needed. Of his forty-three years in Parliament he passed thirty-three as a leader of his political friends, and fourteen years as a Cabinet Minister. Albeit not born to play a part amongst his countrymen, he, by his abiding gifts of intellect and character, reached a pinnacle at which he directed their politics, and for more than a generation was 'the observed of all observers.'"

The *National Zeitung*, the organ of the Right wing of the Liberals, shows an equal appreciation of Lord Beaconsfield's gifts and achievements:—

"Not as Earl of Beaconsfield will his name be handed down by history. A born plebeian, he dies as the Leader of the proudest aristocracy and the prime mover of some of the greatest events in the world. What a career from his first unencouraging reception in the House to the triumphal welcome the nation gave him on his return from the Berlin Congress! Uncommon talent, coupled with the most unflinching will, made him victor in what, at one time, must have appeared the most unequal of contests. As in achieving this extraordinary exploit he had leisure enough to write numerous remarkable novels, in all of which he was his own hero, it is not surprising that he who in life and literature performed such extraordinary feats should have himself become, and is sure to remain, the hero of a large circle of admirers. Whoever may write this wonderful life, be he poet or biographer, will in Disraeli's own writings find the character and objects of the man clearly defined by his own hand. Existence on the heights of society, and the power and notability which it confers, was the aim of his life. Exceedingly clever and firm, and not particularly chary in the choice of his means, he attained his goal in a degree rarely witnessed in modern times."

Prince Bismarck's *Norddeutsche Zeitung* devoted some respectful remarks to the statesman who was a frequent guest at the German Chancellor's house a few years since:—

"The telegraph announces the death of a statesman whose hand has frequently controlled the destinies of his country, and whose history fills a teeming page in the annals not only of England but of Europe and the world at large. Always brilliant and influential, he entered upon the most remarkable period of his life when accepting office in 1874. He purchased the Suez Canal shares to obviate future complications in a particularly important quarter; opposed Russian *prestige* by the creation of the Indian Imperial title; annexed the Transvaal; concluded the Anti-Slavery Convention with Egypt, and formed the South African Confederacy, all of which greatly contributed to raise the power and authority of Great Britain in a new and immense field of action. The diplomatic campaign of the Berlin Congress and the acquisition of Cyprus added fresh successes to his previous political exploits. By his art and tact he managed to make the Balkans the frontier of Bulgaria, to recover the Ægean for Turkey, and to protect Stamboul and satisfactorily settle the question of the Straits. In 1879 he was less fortunate. Though he opened it with the proud dictum, '*Imperium et Libertas*,' the British arms failed to keep what in former times had been so gallantly won in Asia and Africa. Cabul, indeed, was taken, and rebellion quenched at the Cape; but the Irish question assumed a threatening aspect, and a little later the Liberals gained a complete victory in the General Election. Aged, yet active, he retired from office, but not from politics, and he has now departed this life at a moment when he might have hoped by his powerful intelligence and fertility of resource once more to defeat the *disjecta membra* of the Liberal Party. Disraeli is dead, and one of the most prominent politicians and most devoted British patriots has disappeared from the scene."

A like eulogium was bestowed on Lord Beaconsfield by the Government journal, the *Post*:—

"Prince Bismarck always knew a patriot jealous of his country's greatness and might when he met him."

The Austrian and Hungarian press, in fact, lamented the event as though Austria or Hungary herself had lost a leading statesman.

The *Extra-Blatt* expressed itself as follows:—

"The announcement of the death of Earl Beaconsfield has excited the profoundest sympathy throughout the entire world of cultivated society. Queen Victoria never had a more faithful counsellor; nor, since the days of Pitt and Fox, has England ever possessed a more brilliant statesman. It was by his own mental vigour that Disraeli raised himself from obscurity to the highest pinnacle of political eminence and dignity. The statesman and writer of romances, whose eyes are now for ever closed, became long ago, as plain Mr. Disraeli, the leader of the British Conservatives. Bereft of his genius, the party has lost a head which it will be difficult, if not impossible, to replace. When the elections of 1874 carried Disraeli to the Premiership, one result was that the slumbering British lion was roused by the Prime Minister to a consciousness of his great position in the world. To Disraeli it was due, moreover, that the dreams of Ignatieff were not fulfilled, and that the whole of the East did not become a mere appanage of the Cossacks."

The article concluded by noting that "in the decease of Lord Beaconsfield Austria-Hungary loses one who had at all times and in various ways proved her true and faithful friend."

The *Presse* said :—

"To-day Englishmen have to lament the departure of one of their greatest statesmen. Both the great political parties in England will equally feel this severe loss. To the Tories the blow will be the more severe that the Earl has left no one behind him who can replace his authority with the Party, and the question who is to succeed him as the Conservative Leader is one that will be very difficult to determine."

The *Deutsche Zeitung* remarked that

"The British Empire has just lost its most eminent statesman, a man who in many important qualities surpassed even his great antagonist, the present English Premier. It was the departed statesman who for thirty years past led, or shared in leading, the Tory party, shedding upon it the greatest brilliancy, and leading it from impotence to a dazzling lease of power. The death of Disraeli is a loss heavy indeed for England, but for the Conservative Party almost irreparable."

The *Tageblatt*, commenting on the news, expressed its opinion that

"The Earl of Beaconsfield was a great man and a great statesman. For fifty years he has taken part in the public life of England, sometimes in a less prominent position, at others in the foremost ranks. He descends to the tomb in his seventy-seventh year, having attained the highest possible pinnacle of glory open to his ambition. Never had the name of

Beaconsfield filled a larger space in the world, never had he exercised more influence on the destinies of Europe, never had he made a more decided mark on the history of the world, than in the last years of his life. All whose hopes and fears centred upon a change in the policy of England fixed their eye upon Mr. Gladstone's most redoubtable opponent. Firmly as the Tories generally hold together —and they are always far more united than the Liberals—they can scarcely fail to suffer in their stability from this loss, for there is no one to be found who is capable of stepping into the position and wielding the colossal inheritance left behind by this great Party Leader."

The Ministerial *Abend Post* spoke of the telegram from London announcing the death of Earl Beaconsfield as "a mournful message of woe."

"The intelligence of the decease of this celebrated statesman and author excites the deepest sympathy throughout the political and literary world of Europe generally, and of Austria-Hungary in particular, to which this death represents an irreparable loss. In the person of Lord Beaconsfield the Nestor of the Tory statesmen of England is laid in the grave. He was the most illustrious representative of that Party in which he for thirty years held undisputed the post of leader, and for which, with his talents as a parliamentary debater, he achieved with the weapons of the mind the most splendid victories. Europe mourns the departure of a politician endowed with such rare gifts of intellect, and such a sagacious insight into the great problems of the world, while on her own part Austria-Hungary laments the loss of a warm admirer and sincere friend."

The *Neue Freie Presse* declared that "England had lost the greatest of her statesmen, who was not only the undisputed head of the Conservative Party, but, at the same time, an ornament to literature. The importance of the man is seen from the fact that, rising from comparatively modest beginnings, he twice led the Tories to victory, twice guided the helm of the State, and most effectively thwarted Russian policy at the Congress of Berlin. But it is impossible to criticise his work and character in this brief notice. All England applauded Lord Beaconsfield as the chief adviser of Queen Victoria, who described the result of the meeting at Berlin as 'Peace with Honour.' After the elections two years later he fell from power, and gave place to Mr. Gladstone. Since that time Liberal England has suffered only defeats in her foreign policy, while even in its home policy the Liberal Premier has often been more illiberal than the often scolded Imperialist. England will sincerely bewail the loss of this statesman, who was greatly esteemed by the Sovereign, and whom his friends the Conservatives will find it very difficult to replace, as no new leader can possess his undisputed authority. The Liberals themselves acknowledge that by his death England suffers an incalculable loss. For many years the British Empire has possessed no more powerful representative, and no greater champion of its *prestige* in the world, than the Earl of Beaconsfield."

Among papers published in Rome the *Bersaglieri*, in three long columns, traced Lord Beaconsfield's biography eulogistically :—

" His imagination and affections often dominated his intellect. When he was the First Minister of the Empress of the Indies, and champion of England's greatness, he was still, as always, a romancer. His life was a wonderful romance. The son of a Venetian Hebrew, he determined to enter the ranks of the proudest and most powerful aristocracy in the world. He conquered in the struggle, and entered their ranks triumphantly; and this aristocracy acclaimed him its chief, chose him its defender, and implored his consent to allow his plebeian head to be covered with a diadem. The man whom Mr. Gladstone had reproached as not having a drop of English blood in his veins has given to the English Gladstone a terrible lesson in patriotism. He found England reduced, as Lord Russell said, to a power of the third order, and he replaced her in her ancient position. When the plebeian of Maidstone returned from Berlin in 1878, where he had victoriously struggled with the Andrassys, the Gortschakoffs, and the Bismarcks, and was able to say proudly to his nation,

'I bring you peace with honour,' an immense burst of applause was thundered from shore to shore of England. Guided by an ideal higher than that of the politics of the day or the existence of a Ministry, Mr. Disraeli more than once changed his policy. His end was ever the greatness and prosperity of England. To the domesticity-loving Queen this ambitious man, this remoulder of Empires, was extremely dear. The daughter of the Brunswicks and Tudors leaned in glad security on the arm of the Hebrew's son."

The *Diritto* published five large columns containing a careful *résumé* of Lord Beaconsfield's life. To judge of its influence and significance so hurriedly, it says, is difficult. The man appears greater in himself than in what he has done for his country, in which, perhaps, more fame and phosphorescence is to be found than real and durable advantage.

The *Capitan Fracassa* gave two articles occupying several columns, by two writers, one on the Author, and one on the Statesman. The former said:—

"What Dickens did for the middle and lower classes Mr. Disraeli did for the aristocracy. The impression produced in high life by the early romances of the young Jew just escaped from the life of commerce, may be imagined. His latter novels are in fact real political battles, in which vivid fancy and incisive style are the arms employed. One thing strikes and pleases us in all the literary work of Disraeli—namely, his great and efficacious sympathy for the Jews. A wonderful and ever restless genius, he chose to fuse literature and politics, and thus produced romances too much coloured by politics, and followed a political policy too romantic."

The other writer said :—

"He won victory for the Conservatives on three splendid occasions, the grandest of which, perhaps, was the occasion of his Reform Bill. This clever and patriotic act immensely increased his *prestige*, proving him to possess that fundamental quality of every modern statesmen—aversion to dogmatism. His birth, the religion of his fathers, his own story, did not prevent him from triumphing over the prejudices of the British aristocracy against a new man; for the English aristocracy has this wonderful quality which assures the perpetuity of its strength—once it recognises genius, far from combating or avoiding it, it defends, it attracts, it makes it part of itself. Thus it is truly what its name indicates, ' the government of the best.' Thus Mr. Disraeli, instead of becoming a violent Tribune, became the able and successful leader of the aristocracy. This man, whom Mr. Gladstone had reproached as a foreigner, so conducted himself as to become the champion and restorer of the greatness of England. The Gladstone Ministry which fell in 1874 was, save in finance, a notable monument of weakness and improvidence; and England fell very low. Lord

Beaconsfield answered to the cry of Europe too late to prevent the war of 1876; he, however, mitigated its effects, tore up the San Stefano Treaty, saved from Russian domination a great part of the conquered provinces, and gloriously defended Western Europe against the tyranny of the North. Returning from Berlin, he laid at the feet of his Queen the inestimable gem of Cyprus, and answered Russian menaces by inducing Her Majesty to assume the crown of the Indies, as if to show that that country, as an integral part of the British Empire, would be defended with all the power of the English Crown. The people applauded the happy policy of their Minister, and for six years deemed the increased taxation well spent for such objects. Then the money question prevailed, and Lord Beaconsfield fell. Political life is now changed in England. Her old institutions are being destroyed, and amid such a scene Mr. Disraeli would no longer have known his place. He has died in time, leaving the memory of one of the most able and fortunate statesmen Europe has ever seen."

The *Opinione* said :—

"Lord Beaconsfield was not only the head of a great Party, but was truly one of the most remarkable Statesmen recorded in history. His origin might have inclined him to combat the aristocracy; the native instincts of his lofty and superb intellect impelled him rather to impose himself on it, to make himself necessary to it, to assume the direction of it and govern it. Fate reserved for Lord Beaconsfield in his last days great and poignant grief. He was condemned to see his work destroyed by his successor, who voluntarily renounced in Central Asia the scientific frontier of the Indian Empire acquired by so great sacrifices, and in Africa the Transvaal. But Mr. Gladstone cannot injure the literary monument of his great rival, for it is out of his power."

The *Italia* said:—

"His name will remain attached to certain events of altogether special importance, and marked by an excessive boldness. The purchase of the Suez Canal shares is not forgotten, which the country so enthusiastically ratified; and in the last war, who was it that arrested the victors at the gates of Constantinople, despite the violent opposition of Mr. Gladstone and his friends?" The *Italia* concludes a long and appreciative article by saying its imperfect sketch is sufficient to render possible a measurement of the immensity of England's loss.

The *Popolo Romano*, in the course of a long article, wrote:—

"The humble descendent of a Jewish family driven from their refuge at Venice, and then received by hospitable England, raised himself to be the giver of the title of Empress to the Queen of Great Britain, and to add Cyprus to the British Empire. The life of Lord Beaconsfield illustrates one of the most characteristic elements of English political life. He was accused, but his countrymen loved him; abused, but at the same time admired; and public life in England will long feel the absence of that brilliant and unique personality. The author of *Endymion*, and of the annexation of Cyprus, did what he pleased with the British aristocracy. The power of his fascination was unlimited. He led it at his pleasure, notwithstanding that his temperament and that of the Party he guided were at antipodes. Such was the power of attraction exercised by this prodigiously able man, that his adversaries were far from considering his retirement definitive, and therefore all England is now weeping the death of a man who always most sincerely loved her, and ever sought, even if sometimes erroneously, to make her great and respected."

The *Riforma*, Signor Crispi's paper, had a very long article admitting the wonderful power and ability of the late Earl, but speaking grudgingly of his work, and how mistakenly may be estimated by the expressed opinion that Lord Beaconsfield represented the dead Toryism of a past time. Alone in all the press, the *Riforma* thinks the death of Lord Beaconsfield an advantage for England.

The tone of the Russian press was less uniformly favourable. But the semi-official *Journal*, in an article remarkable alike for its good taste and the excellence of its style, said:—

"Whatever may be thought of the foreign policy of Lord Beaconsfield, all recrimination or retrospective criticism must be hushed in the presence of death. Now, too, that cordial relations exist between England and Russia we can survey more calmly and dispassionately the actions of a statesman who, though a prey to prejudice, was animated, doubtless, by the purest patriotism. We cannot forget that Lord Beaconsfield's last effort as an orator was to render homage to our dead Emperor, to express the admiration he felt for the great deeds of his reign, sympathy with Russia in her affliction, execration against the authors of sacrilegious crime. We can sympathise with the grief which the English nation must now experience. England has lost one of her two great Statesmen—the man who is remarkable in more respects than one, whose whole career presents a wonderful intermixture of personal merit, social triumphs, and national gratitude to the Conservative party. The death of Lord Beaconsfield is an irreparable blow. As an historical figure Lord Beaconsfield has a grandeur of his own—a tinge of romance is spread over his whole career. By his genius, stubbornness, and will, he in some sort forced himself upon his countrymen. He dominated circumstances and pressed them into his service. Few men have inspired warmer friendship or intenser hate. His admirers exalted him to the skies, whilst his opponents trailed his name through the mud.

His biographies are panegyrics or satires, and it would seem impossible for his contemporaries to judge him coolly and impartially. His ruling qualities were imagination and sentiment. He loved vast conceptions, and was apt to be led away by grandiose projects. On the other hand, he held in horror all details of routine and mere mechanical work. Whatever opinion one may have of Lord Beaconsfield, it must be confessed that he occupies a great and noble position in the history of his country. We can scarcely think that another Benjamin Disraeli will make his appearance on the world's stage. He who is this day mourned by Englishmen without distinction of opinions presents a figure quite exceptional amongst statesmen whose mames adorn the annals of England."

The *Golos* wrote :—

" From the stage of European politics has passed away one of the greatest and perhaps the most prominent of contemporary Statesmen. The English Conservative Party has lost its leader, the English Parliament one of its most brilliant orators, and Mr. Gladstone his most dangerous opponent. Europe undoubtedly will breathe freer from knowing that those political surprises showered upon her in such abundance during Lord Beaconsfield's final lease of power need no longer be feared. Englishmen will acknowledge him as a great Statesman. They may differ from Lord Beaconsfield ; they may reject his views and opinions regarding many things ; but they are bound to acknowledge his clear mind, resolute character, strong will, and unbounded patriotism. Such, also, is the judgment that Russia must repeat, in spite of the hard time we had to pass through, thanks to the views and tendencies of Lord Beaconsfield."

The *Poriadok* said:—

"The death of Lord Beaconsfield is an event of political importance, not to England alone, but to all Europe. One of England's greatest statesmen, the all-powerful leader of the Tory Party, he was at the same time the best and most talented representative of the old school of politics which is fast losing ground in contemporary Europe. The name of Benjamin Disraeli is inseparably bound up with the history of England, and to write his biography would be to cite all the chief events in the history of his country during the last forty years. The political career of Benjamin Disraeli presents us with much that is instructive. It affords a brilliant proof that the talent and energy of individuals, where public life is allowed, develop themselves freely and attain results which in other circumstances are impossible. The most powerful and enlightened aristocracy in Europe acknowledged as its chief the man who sprang from a modest literary circle. The most brilliant period of Lord Beaconsfield's life was the last decade, in the course of which he secured the triumph of his Party, and in the quality of its Leader showed the way to outward glory and Imperial power. Disraeli contributed greatly to re-establish the political *prestige* of England in Europe and the East. It seemed at one time that he would outshine Bismarck with his daring deeds, such as the annexation of Cyprus and the despatch of the fleet to the Bosphorus. He strengthened and confirmed England's position in India by resolute measures calculated to produce an effect upon Eastern peoples. Queen Victoria was proclaimed Empress of India, and the neighbouring central Asiatic Powers were brought to a state almost of vassalage by means of subsidies and energetic campaigns. This policy of Beaconsfield gave rise to bitter criticism, especially in Russia."

The *Novoe Vremya* said :—

"He stood up for despotism and wrong, and although he obtained a passing success in the struggle with our diplomacy, the English people fell away from their leader. Lord Beaconsfield left no good recollections, either at home or in Russia, against which he cherished enmity and hatred; nor with the Turks, whom he protected. Beaconsfield bore no standard. He was neither the representative of his liberty-loving country, nor the champion of the high eternal principles necessary to the existence of humanity. He was a man of brilliant talent, which was squandered in the service of a degenerate aristocracy, and in the passionate satisfaction of his own insatiable ambition."

The following is from the *ora*, a Greek paper published at Athens, of April 20th, and is written by M. Tricoupis:—

"Greece had not the good fortune to enjoy any great favour in the eyes of the deceased statesman. Although not exactly popular, Lord Beaconsfield was profoundly admired as a genius who had a strong and resolute will. Disraeli was no mere chief at the service of his Party. He was their model, and the source of their great political ideas. His death cannot fail to weaken the vigour of English political life at home as well as British *prestige* abroad. Every one who is convinced that the influence of England upon European politics is beneficent cannot fail to regret the death of the noble Lord, who had laboured so successfully for the power and glory of his country."

Telegraphing from Pesth on the 20th of April, the correspondent of *The Standard* said: "All the papers of this capital to-day teem with reviews of the life of Lord Beaconsfield, and with reflections upon the political consequences of his death. There is not a single journal here that does not speak of the deceased statesman as a true friend to the Kingdom of Hungary. In this country Lord Beaconsfield's anti-Russian policy has ever met with the most enthusiastic approval, a fact which is very intelligible when it is recollected that within the past generation Hungary has had to suffer at the hands of the Muscovites. If any nation has cause to fear for its liberties on account of the proximity and power of Russia, it is the Magyars, who after 1848 were crushed by the mercenaries of the Czar. The ever-present source of danger to Hungarian freedom which is found in the existence of the colossal despotic Empire beyond the Eastern borders of Hungary explains the enthusiastic gratitude with which this country dwells on the services rendered to her by the anti-Slavonic policy of the late Premier of England."

A few days later, April 24th, *The Standard* correspondent at Alexandria telegraphed: "The Khedive expresses his deep regret at the death of Lord Beaconsfield. His Highness declares that he will never forget the kind, conciliatory policy, amounting even to a real friendship, which was inaugurated in Egypt by the great statesman now deceased. That policy, the Khedive added, has greatly contributed to the prosperity and progress of Egypt."

In England itself the manifestations of public sentiment which followed on the news of the death of Lord Beaconsfield were not less remarkable. *The Standard* of the day following that on which the event occurred published three columns of closely printed letter-press, containing accounts of its reception in every part of the United Kingdom. On the whole the country was not unprepared for the announcement, though in some places surprise was mingled with regret. At Manchester, where the bulletins of the previous week had led to a revival of hope, the flags on the roofs of the Conservative and the Liberal Clubs were hoisted half-mast high. At Newcastle-on-Tyne the bell of St. Nicholas' Church was tolled, and the Vicar of Newcastle, at the Easter vestry meeting, spoke at length on the national loss. At Liverpool, where the Conservatives were specially attached to the ex-Premier, and firm admirers of his political career, flags were displayed at half-mast from all the public buildings, while the Mayor decided to postpone his "at home" at the Town Hall, and a banquet at the same place on Friday, for both of which invitations had been issued. At Leeds, by order of Alderman Tatham, the Liberal mayor, the great bell in the Town Hall tower was tolled from ten to eleven o'clock from respect to Lord Beaconsfield's memory. At Plymouth the news was published in second editions of the morning papers. There are few places in which party feeling runs higher than in the great seaport of the West, but the sorrow caused by the death of the leader of the Conservative party was universal. At Bath, where Lord Beaconsfield was a voter till he was struck off the roll on going to the House of Lords, the sentiment was the same. At Birmingham, both at the Conservative and Liberal Clubs, flags were hoisted half-mast. The Exeter newspapers published the telegram in special editions, surrounded by black borders. Flags half-mast floated from several buildings, and at noon the cathedral bell tolled. At Bristol there were the same signs of mourning, and a Conservative meeting called for the evening, which Mr. David Plunket and Mr. H. S. Northcote had promised to attend was postponed. Sheffield, Preston, Wolverhampton, and every country town of any size, joined in the general mourning. The reports from Scotland and Ireland told the same tale. At Edinburgh and Glasgow important meetings were immediately postponed. At Aberdeen touching reference was made at a meeting of the Presbytery to the event. In Dublin, where Lord Beaconsfield's political adherents were very numerous and the ranks of his political opponents included many admirers of his writings; in Limerick, of which place Lord Beaconsfield's physician, Dr. Kidd, is a native; in Belfast, and all the other great centres of the Irish population, no sign of sorrow was wanting.

At the various political meetings, Liberal and Conservative, held during the next few days throughout the country, regretful and sympathetic mention was made of Lord Beaconsfield by the chief speakers, irrespectively of their political views. Lord Lymington, delivering an address at North Tawton on educational energy, dwelt upon the great example offered to the English people in Lord Beaconsfield's career, and upon his consistent display of the characteristics which were always highly appreciated by Englishmen, strong independence of character, strong belief in his own views, and an indifference for the prejudices and casual changes of public opinion. At a dinner of the North Northamptonshire Conservative Association, Lord Burghley referred to the deep gloom which had been cast over the country by the death of Lord Beaconsfield, adding that his advice was of immense importance to the Constitution.

Meetings were held by all the Conservative Associations of the country; and resolutions testifying to the loss sustained were passed. At a meeting of the Plymouth Union of Conservative Associations, Mr. Edward Clarke said of Lord Beaconsfield that he had for six years wielded, with unquestioned authority and with the full consent of the people, the mightiest power which had been enjoyed by an English Minister during the last half century. He never (he added) struck a small antagonist. In all the debates in the House of Commons he attacked the leaders on the opposite side.

At Southport a day or two later (April 23), Lord Lathom spoke of Lord Beaconsfield as a man whose death would be deplored throughout the country, not only by Conservatives, but by Liberals also; adding that he had lost in Lord Beaconsfield a personal and very dear friend of his own. Mr. Walter, at Wokingham, alluded to the death of the distinguished man, "whose form, character, voice, and figure were so distinguished in this country. Whatever difference of opinion there might exist with regard to his conduct and career, they would all agree that the present century had not produced another such phenomenon in English politics. Lord Beaconsfield was a man who, by sheer force and energy, and by undaunted courage and perseverance for over forty years of public career, had forced his way from the very ranks of English public life to the highest position an Englishman can aspire to and a statesman possibly occupy. A career so remarkable was only possible in a country where character and conduct were so strictly, scrupulously, and closely watched."

There were other qualities in Lord Beaconsfield than his genius and success which attracted the English people, and which explain the extraordinary display of national feeling that has just been described. Lord Beaconsfield achieved the fame and influence of a great Statesman, not only by dint of his genius, but by his insight into the character of the race amid whom his lot was cast. If he seemed at times to be a figure removed by some mysterious barrier from the actors in that great drama of affairs in which he bore so prominent a part, it was not because he was unacquainted with the springs of their action or the secrets of their movements. Meditation supplied the incentive and material of performance; observation, matured by reflection, taught him how performance could yield the most enduring results. In the management of mankind, he has said more than once, the force of the imagination as well as the reason must be taken into account. Nor did he recognise in the English nation any exception to this rule. The English people he declared were one of the most emotional and enthusiastic in the world; in the union which Lord Beaconsfield himself presented of the imaginative and the practical there was something which appealed powerfully to the popular feeling. He was not a political philosopher in the sense in which that title might be bestowed on Sir G. Cornewall Lewis, or on Mr. J. S. Mill; but he had a wider, a deeper, and perhaps a more truly philosophic knowledge of the political forces at work than, perhaps, any Statesman of his generation.

In some of his novels Lord Beaconsfield has keenly satirised the mysterious essence known as "the spirit of the age." But there were occasions on which Lord Beaconsfield used the expression with all earnestness, and his whole career was a proof of his accessibility to the influences of the power. "Without," he said in his inaugural address to the Glasgow students in 1873, "an acquaintance with the spirit of the age in which we live, whatever our culture and whatever our opportunities, it is probable that our lives may prove a blunder." Many other persons may have used much the same language, but without signifying the same thing. "The spirit of the age," as Lord Beaconsfield knew it himself, and as he impressed the necessity of its knowledge upon others, was no aggregate of crude abstractions. It was not to be understood by any arbitrary *à priori* process, but by close and patient investigation. It was not the intuition of the philosopher, but the gradual elaboration of the practical student.

One of the secrets of Lord Beaconsfield's greatness and success is unquestionably contained in his own life-long fulfilment of the precept which he impressed with such brilliancy of illustration upon the Scotch undergraduates eight years ago. The vigour and accuracy of Lord Beaconsfield's judgment were, of course, in a large degree the spontaneous results of his own splendid intellect. But he would have employed them with comparatively little effect unless he had made a systematic study of the signs of the times. It may be said of Lord Beaconsfield that in him "old experience did attain to something of prophetic strain;" but it was that experience, the capacity to acquire which was implanted by genius, and strengthened by methodic practice. For these reasons, it may be said of Lord Beaconsfield that no statesman of our times has possessed anything like the same faculty of political prevision. The Tapers and Tadpoles, whom Lord Beaconsfield has pelted with ridicule in *Coningsby*, fancied they could see farther ahead than most people. But it was one thing to be able to apply the measure of the electioneering agent upon any given occasion, and another to be able to gauge the tendencies and the action of public opinion. This art Lord Beaconsfield possessed in an extraordinary degree.

His possession of it was constantly illustrated in two different ways. It prevented him during the whole period that he was responsible for the policy of the Conservative Party from offering an obstinate resistance to measures on which the majority of the English people were bent. The reason why the popularity of Conservatism increased so much under the leadership of Lord Beaconsfield was, that he would never allow Conservatism to adopt an attitude of invidious antagonism to the manifest will of the day. The second mode in which Lord Beaconsfield's rare faculty of political prescience exercised itself was, perhaps, more remarkable. It may never be known whether Lord Beaconsfield was personally surprised at the results of the General Election held last year. It may or it may not be that he had subsequently misgivings as to the tactical wisdom of the letter which, on the eve of the Dissolution, he addressed to the Duke of Marlborough. However that may be, events have since proved the accuracy of the view which he took of the political future of Ireland. The agitation which has since vexed that country has shaped itself upon the same lines which Lord Beaconsfield predicted. More than a decade has passed since *Lothair* saw the light. The novel has its faults; but it is a remarkable commentary on some of those events which have lately harassed Europe. In 1870 the "Secret Societies" of the Continent were merely a name to the ordinary reader. Since then M. Cherbuliez has addressed himself to the theme, and more recently an English novelist has attempted to develop the same idea. "Secret Societies" have now become exactly what, eleven years ago, Lord Beaconsfield led us to expect, and much of what then to many people savoured of Transpontine melodrama might be read now almost as a transcript from contemporary history.

Lord Beaconsfield succeeded also in an unprecedented degree in making every question his own to which he chose to dedicate his genius, and of setting it in a new light unsuspected till then by the ablest and most thoughtful of his contemporaries. He saw that after 1832 the time had arrived for criticising the Revolution settlement of 1688, and it became in his hands the Venetian Constitution. He saw that if the Tory Party was ever to regain its old ascendency in the country it must be by recurring to those principles which had originally made it popular, and eventually rendered it predominant. He referred us, therefore, to the principles professed by that party in the early part of the last century, and to some extent carried out by Mr. Pitt, in preference to any modified version of the debased Toryism which grew up after 1815. When it fell to his lot to deal with Parliamentary Reform, he did not so much endeavour to accommodate representation to numbers — which he saw, perhaps, was a hopeless task without something like a social Revolution—as to ensure that all classes and interests in the country should find proper expression in the House of Commons. The "representation of interests" accordingly became, under his peculiar treatment of it, almost a new idea, and one which unquestionably exercised very considerable influence in the settlement of the Reform Question. His principle of a rate-paying suffrage was calculated to make the representation popular, without making it democratic, by introducing an intelligible principle which should place the exclusion of irresponsible numbers on a national basis, such as public opinion could endorse. But that he induced his followers to accept this doctrine, and that he carried through his great measure of 1867 without endangering the unity of his Party, is a wonderful tribute to the force of his personal character and the spell of his peculiar genius.

It will be interesting to supplement these remarks with a few extracts from the sermons delivered on the Sunday following Lord Beaconsfield's death by well-known clergymen. Canon Prothero, who preached before the Queen at Whippingham Church, taking as his text St. Luke xxiv. 30, said—

"If some sudden trouble have fallen upon you in the loss of a great councillor and supporter, whom in these trying and dark days the nation can ill spare, on whose wisdom and foresight it has long leant and never leant in vain, without whose sagacious counsel the weighty affairs of rule must be very heavy to bear, whose removal from the Senate leaves a blank which cannot at present be filled, still it is only wise, it is only due to our past experience of life, so mercifully ordered by our Heavenly Father, to look back on those many calamities through which we have passed and those which we have been taught to endure, and without expecting to see the why and the wherefore of such sorrows as this one, to trust in Him who has caused them, and who says to us 'Be not faithless, but believing.'"

At Sandringham Church, where the Prince and Princess of Wales were present, the sermon was preached by the Rev. T. Shore, who, taking for his text the 25th chapter of St. Matthew, 15th verse,

"And unto one he gave five talents," concluded with the following remarks :—

" Few indeed there have been this century to whom the words of the text can be more fitly applied than to the illustrious statesman who passed away last Tuesday morning early. The foes of a lifetime and the friends of a lifetime will, no doubt, bear a willing and eloquent tribute to his supreme intellectual capacity, which seemed to create as well as to utilise circumstances. They will do honour to the genius of the dead statesman; but here we will add that with these intellectual endowments there were combined moral qualities not always found in the same connection. His faithful fidelity to friends, a pure and tender respect for woman, a generous and healthful appreciation of younger intellect in life's battle, a courage which rose higher as hope died out in other less brave hearts, a patience which waited in confidence, in silence through years of scorn, a patriotism which in great national crises rose above all mean consideration of party, a passionate jealousy for his country's honour, a loyal and chivalrous devotion to his Queen—these were the moral qualities which characterised a great man's life. The great statesman has died, but the energising power of his life survives. The memory of the first and last Earl of his name will endure as an heritage to coming ages to kindle the genius and to promote the enthusiasm of generations yet unborn."

The Bishop of Liverpool, occupying the Oxford University pulpit at St. Mary's, made a special reference to the death of Lord Beaconsfield :—

" That a great statesman had been removed from them on a day when great statesmen were few appeared to be the common opinion of the world. From north to south and east to west the verdict was the same, the tongue on which listening senates often hung with admiration was at length silent.

The busy mind which coined so many striking thoughts never likely to be forgotten, and devised schemes which affected the future of empires and startled rulers and kings, had at last ceased to work in this world. This was one of those deaths which produced the sensation of a sudden gap or blank being made in the great circle of the human family. About his political opinions that was not the time or place to speak. Of his inner religious life he knew nothing. But he did see in him two striking features of character which he commended to the notice of all who heard him, and he commended them especially to his younger hearers. If ever there was an English statesman who could calmly rally his forces after losing a battle, who courageously began a new campaign and bided his time like Fabius until he marched through repeated defeats to victory, that statesman was Lord Beaconsfield. He had many faults, no doubt, and made many mistakes, for he was only a mortal man; but even his opponents must admit that no political leader had risen so steadily and stemmed the tide so manfully; none had so completely illustrated the old adage, 'All things come to the feet of him who can wait.'"

The Rev. Henry White, chaplain of the Chapel Royal, Savoy, preaching at the noon service in the Chapel Royal, St. James's, from the words, " God's eye beholds every precious thing" (Job xxviii. 10), remarked—

"The pulpit of a Christian sanctuary is not the place where political allusions or personal adulations should be pronounced; but I suppose that a preacher who should shun all reference to the wide-world loss which the utterances of the past week have so abundantly recorded, would fail to meet the appropriate expectations either of this or of any other congregation. During the last five days the columns of every English and foreign journal have been crowded with ample accounts of that great career which closed at the dawn of day last Tuesday, within the distance of a few paces from this chapel. Of his consummate genius as an author, as an orator, as a statesman, there have been and there will yet be plentiful testimonies. Perhaps it may best suit the place and the occasion this morning to bear some witness to the worth and the wealth of his personal fidelities and friendships. Even those who had the slenderest opportunities of knowing him in his own home can remember how touching it was to watch the vehement, fiery Parliamentary gladiator enjoying the sunshine of domestic life with her who was to him the most tender, devoted, and self-sacrificing wife that any man could desire or deserve. I see that there are some in this chapel who can remember that on the Sunday after her funeral he came to the Savoy Chapel and stood, or knelt, with head and heart bowed in grief. Nor can I forget the kindly appreciation which he felt, and referred to, of many words in the hymns and in the sermon which, by a strange coincidence quite unpremediated, were in sympathy with his sorrow and the bereavement he had recently suffered. A little while later on, and soon after his last assumption of office, he offered to one destitute of any claims on his patronage, and quite spontaneously, a distinguished and responsible office, and even added to this kindness the oft-repeated regret that the responsibility was not undertaken. These personal reminiscences are utterly valueless in themselves, but they bear witness to that tender and loyal devotion which marked in unerring course all his private and public life. Whatsoever may be the verdict of posterity, whatsoever may be said hereafter of this illustrious man—the most searching and cynical criticism will not be able to deny that, despite all the failings and faults to which the most exalted characters are not strangers, there met in him an array of intellectual gifts, of brilliant attainments, of loyal attachment to his Sovereign, to his country, to his friends, which only a few of his contemporaries have ever reached or rivalled."

At St. Paul's Cathedral, at the afternoon service, the Rev. Canon Liddon preached a sermon on the 17th verse of the 24th chapter of St. Luke—" And He said unto them, What manner of communications are these that ye have one to another, as ye walk, and are sad?"

"Since last Sunday a great blank has been created in English public life by the disappearance from among us of a prominent and remarkable figure, who beyond question, filled all but the largest place in the public eye. This is not the time or place for touching, even remotely, upon many questions that are suggested by his career—questions which have already been largely and variously discussed in the public press, and which will continue, no doubt, to be matters of controversy for some time to come. All will agree that his abilities were of the very highest order, that he rose to the foremost position in public life with a rapidity and success almost, if not quite, without a parallel in our history, and that he has left his mark upon our country and upon Europe traced in characters which will not soon be effaced."

The Rev. Canon Farrar, at the first of a series of special Sunday evening services to be held in the nave of Westminster Abbey, selected as his text the 38th verse of the third chapter of the Second Book of Samuel, " Know ye not that there is a prince and a great man fallen this day in Israel?" Canon Farrar said a common loss had befallen England in the death of that great statesman who, full of years and honours, passed to his rest five days ago.

" To-day, as was said at the death of Sir Robert Peel, 'all England feels like one family.' Political animosities, religious animosities were forgotten beside his open grave. Distinctions of Liberal and Conservative, of High and Low Churchmen, were obliterated in the sense of common regret. We no longer thought of old hostilities of policy and severities of language. The dead statesman erred, as we all did. He was the first to acknowledge it. 'I have spent many years,' he said, 'in political life;' and he added, with generous humility, 'I have during that time done many things which I regret, and said many things which I deplore.' He would have been the last to desire the language of indiscriminate eulogy. He would have held, with the poet—

> 'That man was vain, and false as vain,
>   Who said, were he ordained to run
>   His long career of life again,
>   He would do all that he had done.'

"The statesman who had just died was exposed, almost even to the last, to storms of passionate obloquy; yet now the nation claimed him as her own, and would gladly have laid him in that pre-eminently sacred spot where her patriots slept. In no other cemetery in the world did so many great citizens lie in so narrow a space. Chatham was there; and Fox, and Pitt, and Mansfield, and Grattan, and Castlereagh, and Canning, and Wilberforce, and Palmerston; and these, great as they were, would have welcomed him. Lord Beaconsfield had been happy in the opportuneness of his death. He died on the very day on which, a year before, he had resigned to the Queen the seals of that office in which he achieved so splendid a renown. He died a natural death, in old age, and in the zenith of his honours—in a day of peace, with dear friends by his side, and amid the generous regrets of all his contemporaries; and posterity, which saw all things in the slow results of their ripening, would declare that he was not unworthy, had he so desired, to have been laid among those graves over which towered the stately monument of Chatham. History would record, on her dispassionate page, that Lord Beaconsfield consolidated and cheered in defeat, and guided to victory and inspired with a wider policy and with less timid aims, a great Party, which, whether we might belong to it or not, was necessary to the State; that he gave to England a stronger footing in Egypt and the Mediterranean; that he rekindled in her the old sense of her Imperial destinies; that in days when we were almost insolently taunted with our military impotence he inspired us with the old belief in our hitherto unconquered grandeur; and that he made the voice of England heard at the council board of nations as clearly and as commandingly as it had been aforetime. By the grave of Benjamin Disraeli envy herself would admit that there was much room for honest praise. Was it not, for instance, brave and noble in him to stand by his race—to shrink in nowise from the name of Jew, to meet with open scorn the sneers of those who scoffed at what he deemed to be a glory? Might a respectful word not be said, also, about that honourable domestic faithfulness—that loyal love and life-long devotion of kindness and gratitude to the partner of his years—which were often wanting in meaner men? Might we not admire, again, his almost invariable good humour, his kindness to the young, his sympathy with those who differed from him in opinion, and, especially in his later years, the dignity of his reticence under injuries—under attacks of the most envenomed bitterness? Again, it must be admitted that it was one of Lord Beaconsfield's principles—and a very noble one —never to stoop for or hunt after popularity. 'They say— what say they? Let them say,' was a motto which suited his strong self-reliance; and in one of his latest speeches he expressed his contempt for that incessant babblement of crude condemnations—that 'weak, washy, everlasting flood' of dogmatism—on matters of which the writers were profoundly ignorant, and which he characteristically called the 'harebrained chatter of irresponsible frivolity.'"

The following Sunday, May 1st, Dean Stanley, in his sermon in Westminster Abbey, dwelt on the same theme:—

"'Popular judgments' were at all times worthless in themselves. They were echoes, not voices, and breathed in an atmosphere around them which might be turned to good or evil by those who had the arrangement of human affairs, but they had over and over again been proved to shift with every gust of feeling or passion. Such, in a great measure, were the varying opinions respecting the great statesman who has gone. There was the expression of strong approval three years ago; there was the expression of no less strong disapproval a year ago; there is, again, this strong expression of sympathy now which seems almost universal. There was beyond question," continued the Dean, " a great gulf and void created whenever we lost from amongst us any one who had filled a vast space in the eyes of our own and of other countries. It disturbed the balance of power and of parties, changed the hopes and fears of almost every class, and it was not only in the camp to which the departed statesman belonged that this sense of vacancy would be felt. Great statesmen, the acknowledged leaders of parties, were, by the very fact of their greatness, raised above those parties themselves; they were in fact much more nearly allied to each other in purpose and in principle than the ordinary commonplace herd, the rank and file of their supporters, would suffer us to believe." The Dean described Mr. Gladstone and the late Lord Beaconsfield as the " great twin brethren of our day," each supplying what the other needed for the public weal. " Though they differed so widely in opinions, let us hope that posterity will acknowledge that each fought for what he deemed right in the cause of England's empire and of England's commonwealth. The name of Lord Beaconsfield would be remembered by posterity as that of one who had an extraordinary career, which led the alien in race, the despised in debate, the eccentric in demeanour, the romantic adventurer, the fierce assailant, by unflagging perseverance, unfailing sagacity, unshaken fidelity, by constantly increasing dignity, by large and larger breadth of view, to reach the highest summits of fame and splendour."

The feelings of grief at the death of Lord Beaconsfield which the Jewish community, apart from those shared in common with all other Englishmen, specially feel, both on account of the Jewish birth of the deceased statesman, and of his life-long sympathy with the race from which he sprang, found expression in the pulpits of several Jewish synagogues on Saturday, April 23rd, as well as on the previous Wednesday (the day after the death of Lord Beaconsfield, and the seventh day of the Feast of Passover). The Rev. Dr. Hermann Adler, who is acting as Suffragan to his father, the Chief Rabbi, referred to the loss which the country had sustained in the death of the statesman whom, he said, everybody, whatever be their political bias, must acknowledge to have been gifted with brilliant powers, with rich experience, and with far-reaching wisdom :—

"Jews, remembering that Lord Beaconsfield once belonged to their own faith, must, after studying his career, writings, and utterances, readily admit that he never spoke or acted like a renegade, villifying the faith he had forsaken, or contemning the stock whence he had sprung. No Israelite had ever borne more fervent testimony to the sublimity of the religion by which the Hebrew was sustained amid all his persecutions. No one could have uttered more persuasive words or adopted wiser measures to remove restrictions from which the Jews in England, as well as their brethren in the East, had been suffering. Jews could not but record their gratitude to him who had so faithfully served his country, and whose name would be inscribed in the deathless roll consecrated by England's greatest sons."

The Rev. Professor Marks, preaching, at the Synagogue in Upper Berkeley Street, on the destiny of the Jewish race, observed that

"Though the distinguished statesman who had just passed away was, by force of circumstances over which he had no control, driven in his childhood from the ancestral pale of faith, still it was scarcely possible to contemplate his life and to read his works without arriving at the conclusion that up to the last he was susceptible of a pleasurable sentiment at having been born of the race invested with so holy a mission, and for which so great a future lay in store."

During the service at the Central Synagogue, Great Portland Street, the Rev. A. L. Green spoke of the death of Lord Beaconsfield as a great national misfortune :—

"The whole civilised world (he said) was deploring, as all English persons did with all their hearts, as loyal subjects of the Queen, the death of one of the foremost statesmen in the world, who in his life followed the greatest teaching of their faith in its relation to mankind. Whatever might be the condition of Jews, although they might be degraded politically, they could not be demoralised. There was no instance of any man, a Jew, ever having joined a revolutionary party in any State in which he happened to live, however much they had been deprived of their political rights and the rights of common justice. Some of the most able statesmen whom the world had produced had been Jews. Even with all the bigotry of Ferdinand and Isabella, the only man capable of conducting the affairs of State was a Jew. Then again, there were the cases of Crémieux in France and Lasker in Prussia. He wished with all his heart that they could have numbered Benjamin Disraeli as an adherent member of their faith, but it was not his fault that he was not so, but the fault of his family. They could not but think of the genius of the man who, a Jew, with all the prejudices which existed against Jews forty years ago, had succeeded in fighting, by the powerful strength of his genius alone, his way to the leadership not of a Radical Party—he did not desire to speak politically—but of a Conservative Party of this great Conservative country. There was scarcely a parallel instance to be found anywhere. Thanks to Sir David Salomons and Baron Lionel de Rothschild, the avenues to political power were now open to Jews; and here they had had an instance of what the Jew could do. The Master of the Rolls was an earnest Jew, and he was none the less a good judge. They mourned as Jews and as Englishmen the loss which the nation had sustained, in the belief that they would never find Minister or public servant more upright and true than was the late Benjamin Disraeli."

## IV.

### THE FUNERAL.

As soon as the first shock caused by the announcement of the death of Lord Beaconsfield had a little subsided, speculation and inquiry became active as to whether a national tribute to his memory was to be paid in the form of a public funeral. A general impression unquestionably existed that his remains would be laid in Westminster Abbey. It was indeed understood that Lord Beaconsfield's desire was to be buried by the side of the Viscountess Beaconsfield in the quiet parish churchyard at Hughenden. But it was remembered that a desire for private interment had also been expressed by Lord Palmerston, and had been overruled by the will of Her Majesty. The best commentary on the public wish and expectation is the following correspondence:—

"HAWARDEN CASTLE, *April* 19, 1881.

"Dear Lord Rowton,—It was with sad surprise after more favourable accounts of successive days down to yesterday morning that I learned this day at an early hour the decease of Lord Beaconsfield, which will be regarded with so much mournful interest throughout the country and beyond its limits.

"In conformity with the message I have already sent, I desire at once to inform you and his executors, that if it should be agreeable to their wishes, I shall be prepared to give the necessary directions for a public funeral.

"In tendering this honour on the part of the Government I feel assured that I am acting in conformity with the general expectation and desire.

"I remain, dear Lord Rowton,
"Faithfully yours,
"W. E. GLADSTONE.

"P.S.— Should the proposal be accepted, I beg you at once to convey the intimation to my private secretary, Mr. E. W. Hamilton, now in Downing Street."

In acknowledgment of this communication, the following telegram from the Executors of his Lordship's will was at once despatched:—

"*April* 20, 1881.
"From Sir Nathaniel de Rothschild and Sir Philip Rose to the Right Hon. W. E. Gladstone, M.P., Hawarden.

"With deep and sincere appreciation of the generous motives which dictated your offer, we feel ourselves precluded by the terms of Lord Beaconsfield's will from accepting the public mark of honour which you so kindly propose, and have written you fully."

The above telegram was succeeded by the following letter:—

"1, GROSVENOR GARDENS, *April* 20, 1881.

"Dear Mr. Gladstone,—Your letter to Lord Rowton of yesterday has been placed in the hands of myself and Sir Philip Rose, as the executors named in the will of Lord Beaconsfield, and we desire to express our deep sense of the generous motives which have induced you to propose to do honour to his memory by offering to give directions for a public funeral.

"But while fully appreciating this proposal on your part, and expressing our grateful acknowledgment of the terms in which the proposal is conveyed, we feel ourselves precluded from accepting it by the terms of Lord Beaconsfield's will, dated in 1878, and which, so far as regards the directions for his funeral, is an echo of a previous one made in 1873, which directs that he should be buried at Hughenden, by the side of the late Viscountess Beaconsfield, and for which he had made careful provision in his lifetime.

"We fully sympathise with the strong feeling that everywhere exists in favour of a public expression of regret for so great a loss to the country, a feeling which your kind letter anticipated, but we think you will agree with us, upon perusal of the extract from Lord Beaconsfield's will, which I enclose, that we have no alternative but to carry out his wishes.

"I remain, dear Mr. Gladstone,
"Yours faithfully,
"N. M. DE ROTHSCHILD.

" The Right Hon. W. E. Gladstone, M.P."

The following is the extract in question from the will of the Earl of Beaconsfield, dated 16th December, 1878 :—

"I desire and direct that I may be buried in the same vault, in the churchyard of Hughenden, in which the remains of my late dear wife, Mary Anne Disraeli, created in her own right Viscountess Beaconsfield, were placed, and that my funeral may be conducted with the same simplicity as hers was."

It subsequently appeared that there was practically an insuperable obstacle to the burial of the Earl of Beaconsfield in Westminster Abbey. In the will of the late Mrs. Brydges Willyams of Torquay, who bequeathed him her fortune of forty thousand pounds, there was a condition that she should be buried side by side with him. Her remains were laid in Hughenden churchyard, in the tomb where Lady Beaconsfield was subsequently interred, and in which a vacant space was reserved for his Lordship. As further proof that Lord Beaconsfield designed that Hughenden should be his place of sepulture, a member of the firm which supplied the granite work for his wife's tomb states that when carving the central panel, space was reserved for his Lordship's name by special instruction.

The commentary of *The Standard*, April 21, on the correspondence, was as follows :—" The expression of the national desire that Lord Beaconsfield should receive the honour of a public funeral, and that his remains should find a resting place in Westminster Abbey, followed immediately upon the announcement of his death. Both wishes were anticipated with a promptitude which will be cordially welcomed by the English people. Dean Stanley lost no time in requesting Lord Beaconsfield's representatives to sanction his interment within the precincts of the historic shrine which contains the ashes of so many of England's greatest sons. The Prime Minister displayed a not less laudable alacrity. Immediately on hearing the news of Lord Beaconsfield's death, he telegraphed to Lord Rowton his willingness to give the necessary directions for a public funeral. This message was followed by a letter from Mr. Gladstone, which we print this morning, and which will be read with genuine satisfaction by the English people. It is, indeed, only such a tribute as the Premier might be expected to pay to the memory of his illustrious rival who has 'gone before.' Its language is graceful, generous, and judicious, and the significance of the Prime Minister's offer is deepened by the statement of his belief that 'in tendering this honour on the part of the Government he is acting in conformity with the general expectation and desire.' Death, which is the great leveller, is also the great reconciler, and Mr. Gladstone has done well in showing that the long-standing differences between Lord Beaconsfield and himself are closed for ever. There will be only one wish among the English people—that the Prime Minister's proposal may be accepted. The rest of the correspondence shows that there is some doubt whether this will be possible. As soon as they had seen Mr. Gladstone's letter to Lord Rowton, Sir Nathaniel de Rothschild and Sir Philip Rose telegraphed their grateful appreciation of the offer, but added that they did not feel themselves in a position to avail themselves of it. In the will made by him in December, 1878, Lord Beaconsfield 'desires and directs' that he should be buried in the same vault, in the churchyard of Hughenden, in which the remains of Lady Beaconsfield were placed, and that his 'funeral may be conducted with the same simplicity as hers was.' Lord Rowton went to Osborne yesterday and had an interview with the Queen. We may fairly assume that among the subjects mentioned by Her Majesty were the place of Lord Beaconsfield's interment, and the character of his obsequies. If it should be the express will of the Sovereign that the late Earl should be buried in Westminster Abbey, and that his remains should be followed to the grave with all the solemn splendour of a State pageant, it may not be easy for his executors to refuse compliance with the suggestion. The directions in the will must be taken in conjunction with the declaration of the Royal pleasure. Should this course be followed, precedent for it will not be wanting. Lord Palmerston left instructions analogous to those contained in the will of Lord Beaconsfield, and was buried in Westminster Abbey. Whatever responsibility there is in this matter rests with Lord Beaconsfield's representatives, who know perfectly well what, under certain conditions, he would have wished. If they decide that a public funeral and a grave in the great national fane are not in violation of the spirit of Lord Beaconsfield's desires, the English people will be deeply gratified."

The next day the public learned, not without some sense of disappointment, that Lord Beaconsfield's executors had definitely declined the offer made by Mr. Gladstone, and that the departed statesman was to be buried in the quiet churchyard of Hughenden. Lord Beaconsfield's testamentary wishes, expressed in writing between two and three years ago, were to be respected to the letter. . It had seemed possible that as Lord Beaconsfield was understood to have said nothing definitely on this subject during his last illness, the wishes of the Sovereign, and the unquestionable desire of the English people, might have prevailed against the instructions which he had drawn up in 1878. In these matters the testator always knows that he must leave something to the discretion of his executors. Circumstances may have a modifying influence upon instructions of this character, and the latitude of action which the deceased has given to his representatives must be employed in the manner which they believe to be, on the whole, most in harmony with the spirit of his desires. That is the principle on which the executors of Lord Beaconsfield have now acted. The simple fact that the noble Earl did not really cancel the directions of his will before he died may be accepted as conclusive proof that he adhered to them. He must have known perfectly well that the Abbey and a public funeral were within his reach, and his silence on the subject makes it clear that he wished for neither. Not merely on grounds of local memories and personal affection is it natural that Lord Beaconsfield should have contemplated being laid in the same tomb as that by which he stood as chief mourner eight years ago. There is much in the tranquillity and solitude of the spot which may well have had a charm for him. Peel sleeps peacefully in the churchyard of Drayton; the remains of the late Lord Derby are in the vault at Knowsley; Lord Russell is buried at Chenies. The graves of these worthies of our century are not the less honoured or famous because they lie far outside the Abbey Church of Westminster.

The exact order of events was as follows :—On Wednesday, April 20, Lord Rowton went to see the Queen at Osborne. He did not return to London till next day, and it was on the afternoon of that day that the first intimation of the decision as to the place and mode of burial was made. Lord Rowton then explained to Sir Nathaniel de Rothschild and Sir Philip Rose, in a conversation at half-past two o'clock, that Her Majesty was anxious not to interfere in the slightest degree with the wishes of the deceased statesman, as set forth in his will with regard to his funeral. Immediately after this interview the following notice was issued:—" We are requested to state that the funeral of Lord Beaconsfield will take place at Hughenden on Tuesday next at 3.30 P.M. In accordance with the wishes clearly expressed by his Lordship, the funeral will be conducted with the same simplicity as that of the late Viscountess Beaconsfield." This notice was the next day supplemented by another to the following effect:—" Lord Beaconsfield's executors desire to announce that, in deference to the wishes so clearly expressed by his Lordship, his funeral will be conducted as privately as possible, and the admissions to Hughenden Manor will necessarily be extremely limited. Inasmuch, however, as many of Lord Beaconsfield's friends may desire to be present at the ceremony, which will take place in the churchyard at half-past three o'clock on Tuesday afternoon, the executors think it right to state that the Great Western Railway Company have made arrangements to run special trains from Paddington on that day, of which particulars may be obtained at the Paddington station."

Pending the arrangements for the funeral, Lord

Beaconsfield's body lay in the back drawing-room where he died, and where he usually transacted business. The coffin was in the centre of the apartment resting upon trestles, beneath which was spread a carpeting of black cloth. The coffin was covered with flowers and wreaths. One of these garlands was conspicuous for the following inscription:—"The last token of respect and admiration and gratitude to the noble Earl of Beaconsfield from one, hours of whose life he has charmed from her earliest years by the magic of his pen." In many cases those who brought the wreaths begged that they might be allowed to place them upon the coffin themselves, but no one was permitted to pass into the front drawing-room, into which the coffin was moved after it had been sealed up. Many neat wreaths were accompanied by cards bearing verses or touching inscriptions. Some coming from little children had most affecting words attached to them, as was the case with others coming from veterans of the political or social world. Among the most artistic of these tributes was an entablature of over two feet in diameter with a double row of white camellias encircling a background of stephanotis, with the words "In Memoriam" worked in violets. As they arrived, the flowers were carefully packed ready for removal with the coffin to Hughenden. Telegrams of condolence and sympathy were hourly received in Curzon Street from every quarter of the globe, many of the potentates of Europe not only sending their messages through their representatives, but also by direct communications. Amongst the messages was one from Prince Bismarck, who expressed his great sorrow at the loss sustained not only by the nation but by the whole Continent. Other leading European statesmen sent telegrams to the same effect.

The final sight of the body of Lord Beaconsfield was taken on Friday, April 22. The features were unchanged; the same tranquil look, which almost became a contented smile, and which had settled on the rigid countenance a few minutes after death, was still visible. Between ten and eleven o'clock on Saturday morning several of the servants left for Wycombe, and were followed shortly before five in the afternoon by Sir Philip Rose, Sir Nathaniel de Rothschild, and Lord Rowton, who at once drove to the Manor. Throughout the whole evening everything remained quiet in the neighbourhood of Curzon Street, and at eleven o'clock the gas was turned down and the house apparently left to repose. About twelve o'clock Mr. Alfred Rothschild arrived. An hour later a hearse, drawn by a single horse, and accompanied by about a dozen undertakers' men, drove into Curzon Street, and the outer coffin destined to receive the shell and lead case in which the remains lay was taken into the house. A few minutes afterwards the coffin was placed in the hearse, which was then at once driven to the Paddington station. At twenty-five minutes past two on Sunday, April 24, the train left for Wycombe. Wycombe was reached in a little under an hour. Quietly, but with the same celerity that had characterised the movements at Paddington station, the hearse was duly horsed and driven off, followed by two flys that had been hurriedly engaged, along Castle Street and through Frogmore Gardens, into the Hughenden Road, entering the grounds of the Manor, nearly two miles distant from the station, by what is locally known as the "Green Lodge." This lodge was erected under the immediate direction of the late Countess, and was one of the last improvements upon the estate suggested by her. When the lodge gates were thrown open the hearse ascended the hill, passing through the "Golden Gates," and so by the Italian Garden to the front of the house. Here the executors, accompanied by Lord Rowton, were in waiting to receive the remains. Just at this moment the first dawn of morning light broke through the clouds, and the birds began their early matin carol, the twittering of the larks and sparrows being answered by the hoarse screech of one of the peacocks that even then had begun to strut around the lawn. In the grey glimmer of daylight, fighting as it was with the glare of the lamps in the hall, the body of the departed statesman was lifted from the hearse and carried into the hall, where it was placed upon a small wheeled bier, draped in black cloth, that had been brought down for the purpose. The coffin was afterwards removed to the centre of the room, which overlooks the Italian Garden that was the favourite walk of Lord Beaconsfield. Immediately behind the head of the coffin hung the portrait of Her Majesty, presented to her trusted adviser by the Queen some years since, while on his left was the likeness of his wife.

Sunday, April 24th, was a memorable day at Hughenden. The picturesque little church of St. Michael's had been made the scene of much loving labour in view of Eastertide. The font was filled with white and green hyacinths, noon daisies, Gueldre roses, and fern leaves. Pulpit and lectern were adorned with primroses, yellow daffodils, and interwoven mosses. The chancel railing was decked in greater variety of colour, artistically blended, the top forming a bed of green, in which azaleas, tulips, violets, primroses, and hyacinths, grouped with charming effect, while handsome potted plants flanked the altar on either side. On the reredos were crosses and other emblems formed with white and pink geraniums and azalea blossoms, while beneath the window suitable texts were embroidered in white on a crimson ground. For the morning service some of these were removed, but enough remained to produce an effect of a most agreeable kind. Before the service commenced, at half-past ten, Lord Rowton, Sir N. M. de Rothschild, and Sir P. Rose came from the house of mourning and took their places in the pew of the late Earl, which was within the chancel screen and behind the choir on the north side. The sermon was preached by the Vicar of Hughenden, who preached from 2 Corinthians xv. 36.

"No doubt," he said, "there are many amongst those whom I am addressing who have known the genial kindness and simplicity with which Lord Beaconsfield was always ready to enter into everything that had to do with the parish. Have we not here watched him coming down, even when at the height of his prosperity and power—coming down here, simply and humbly, Sunday after Sunday, as often as his health permitted, to take his place amongst us, and worship God—joining in our service. Again, do we not remember, many of us, how we, in large numbers, knelt side by side with him only on Christmas Day last at yon altar, where he received from my hand the blessed body and blood of Christ. Knowing him as we did here in Hughenden, no man can say that he was either an irreverent or an irreligious man without most cruelly and most foully maligning his memory. I cannot, I do not, pretend to say that I enjoyed his confidence, or anything like great intimacy with him. I only know this from the necessary intercourse I have had with him as vicar of the parish for twelve years; and I never in my life heard him breathe a syllable which could be construed into irreverence or want of due regard for the Church, whose constitution he so well understood, and whose place and importance in the nation none valued more highly than he did."

On Tuesday afternoon, in weather which happily did not realise the sinister promise of the morning, Lord Beaconsfield's remains were committed to the earth in Hughenden churchyard. The ceremony was deeply impressive and perfectly ordered. Lord Beaconsfield was buried simply, as he wished to be, and the rite was solemn, precisely because it was simple. The appearance which the terminus of the Great Western Railway at Paddington presented on the morning of the day was one of extraordinary activity. Long before the departure of the ordinary 8.25 a.m. train the platform was thronged with persons, many of whom had taken tickets over-night for High Wycombe in order to be in time to witness the final ceremony at Hughenden. The first of the special trains, which started at 10.55 from the middle departure platform, conveyed about 500 passengers; but the demand for room was so pressing that many ticket-holders had to be left behind and content themselves with waiting for the ordinary eleven o'clock train.

The Prince of Wales left shortly after one o'clock, and about twenty minutes later there steamed out of Paddington station a train conveying many members of both Houses of Parliament to Wycombe. The number of persons who actually proceeded to High Wycombe by the Great Western trains during the morning was 1,400; being 300 first-class, 300 second-class, and 700 third-class passengers, together with 100 invited guests.

The railway station of High Wycombe is distant from the Manor House of Hughenden rather more than two miles. For the space of about eight hours every inch of the road was packed by a continuous line of human beings, sometimes three or four, sometimes six, seven, and eight deep. From the early forenoon till close upon three o'clock there was an incessant tide of carriages of every description ebbing and flowing between the opposite columns of spectators. Then a change suddenly came over the spirit of the scene; the traffic stopped; the multitude was hushed in silence, and the stillness was only broken by the tolling of the bell from Hughenden Church tower. Nothing could have been more impressive than the series of contrasts to be encountered between the church and the station. In the town of High Wycombe itself many of the shops were completely closed, and the windows of those which were left open were partially veiled by shutters. The brightness of the day, the clearness of the atmosphere, the tender, hopeful tints visible on the trees in the foreground, were out of harmony with the gloom of the occasion. The broughams, victorias, flys, and other vehicles constantly driven past at a brisk pace filled the air with the echoes of their rattle. The sunshine illuminated with all the colours of the rainbow the water in the fountain that played hard by the Market-place. But as one went further onwards, one might have been conscious of a change in the genius of the place. The same crowd still edged the road—stretched itself, after the town was left behind, under the hedges bursting into verdure and into blossom, and covered the brink of the turf whose undulations reach from the Park gates to the house itself.

But while the scene below—in the pleasant valley traversed by the waters of "that ancient river Kishon," as Lord Beaconsfield loved to call the familiar stream—is one of animation, it soon begins to deepen into solemnity on the road which runs through the Park above. The carriages go at a pace which becomes slower and slower; the air becomes more perceptibly hushed; the concourse of persons of all ages and of all conditions of life is as dense as ever. Here on the hill is a vast multitude collected together. The men and women who compose it are almost without an exception habited in black. They gaze intently, but say nothing. A few minutes more and we pass beneath what Lord Beaconsfield usually spoke of as the "Golden Gates." A sharp turn now in the path which threads the labyrinth of shrubs, and the country house of the departed statesman rises directly in front. The scene is full at every turn of beauty and of natural brightness, and the latter quality is perhaps intensified by the solemnity and the stillness in which everything is steeped. The carriages go quickly up to the front door, outside which two policemen are stationed. The visitors enter and find themselves in a suite of rooms crowded with some of the most famous of living Englishmen, yet devoid even of that buzz of suppressed conversation which it is almost impossible to avoid when such a multitude is gathered together.

It is now a few minutes after three. The Prince of Wales and his brothers arrived a quarter of an hour earlier, but are not in any of the reception-rooms down stairs. The coffin lies on its bier in an alcove leading out of the modest hall of Hughenden Manor. But of its material, one might almost say of its dimensions, nothing can be seen. It is literally one mass of floral beauty. Here are wreaths from every member of the Royal Family in England—bouquets of primroses sent by the Queen, with an inscription attached to them, saying that they came from Osborne Hill, and that they are of the sort which Lord Beaconsfield loved. Here are garlands of gardenias and camellias, of rose-buds and Lent lilies, of crocus, and hyacinth, and daffodil. The windows are open. A perfect concert of bird melody pours in through them, and that music is the only sound audible. The atmosphere is charged with a mixture of sweet, pure odours; the interior of the house is bathed in sunlight; the general impression conveyed is one of peaceful and picturesque beauty. But what really strikes one most is the intense silence. In the library and the drawing-room —which are on the left of the hall, the dining-room lying on the right—there cannot be fewer than two or three hundred gentlemen. But their footsteps make no sound on the surface of the rich velvety carpets, and they pass to and fro without a noise of any kind. They recognise each other by a look; they shake hands, but not a word is said. The effect of all this is something more than powerful. As each visitor enters the drawing-room he is received by Lord Rowton, who utters, however, only a few words, and those with baited breath. Ambassadors, statesmen, diplomatists, cabinet ministers, past, present, and future; country gentlemen who years ago occupied a seat in the House of Commons, but who have since retired, and who have probably no intention of returning to parliamentary life; professional men, —doctors, lawyers, and *littérateurs*—are all here together. Lord Dufferin has come fresh from St. Petersburg; the Duke of Marlborough has hurried over from Biarritz; Lord Hartington arrived an hour ago by the Royal train from Paddington—as did Lord Lytton, Lord Beauchamp, Count Münster and a host of others. It is, as a glance in any quarter will show, a company of mourners, but it is also a company of celebrities.

There is yet half an hour before the funeral procession will start for Hughenden Church, which lies away yonder to the right, almost in a direct line with the house, just outside the park, and on the dip into the valley through which the little stream makes its way. The hall, as has been already explained, leads right through the building, which is of no great depth, and indeed principally consists of frontages. We enter from one lawn, and we pass on to another —that from which the prospect of the town of High Wycombe is commanded. A beautifully kept expanse of soft luxurious turf it is, dotted with trees, and with here and there a flower bed. To-day, however, it is studded with frequent groups of gentlemen, all of them more or less distinguished. They pace up and down, engage with subdued voices in conversation, indicate to each other the chief beauties in the landscape, and now and again glance up at the closed windows of the little room above the porch in which Lord Beaconsfield loved to sit, and where his body till yesterday lay. That room was his sanctuary, and its windows face what he called the Italian Garden. It has been said that the flower beds are not very numerous or extensive. Yet it is known that Lord Beaconsfield loved flowers. Why are there not more of them? The answer to this question comes in the notes of a shrill, weird, penetrating scream from the birds of Juno, which promenade on the lawn in all the pride and plenitude of their magnificence, and with an air which betokens some resentfulness at the intrusion. Years ago, Lord Beaconsfield was told that his peacocks would be fatal to his flowers. "Well, then," he replied, "of the two I prefer the peacocks." The cry of these magnificent fowls is very remarkable, and has about it not a little of eeriness. It is not so much the note of a bird as a wail and a death dirge.

It is now within a few minutes of half-past three, and the company collected on the lawn becomes aware, though no specific intimation of the fact has been conveyed to it, that the funeral procession is about to form. All is done silently and in perfect order. There seems to be no necessity for instructions audibly delivered at the last moment; there is no confusion, no uncertainty as to the place which is to be filled by individual mourners, no inconvenient crowding, no unseemly excitement. Everything is dignified, impressive, tranquil, decorous, and solemn. Slowly, and amid the same ever-pervading stillness, though in the presence of tens of thousands of spectators, the coffin is borne down the road which leads from the gravelled walk that runs round the front lawn to Hughenden Church. The Bucks Volunteers are drawn up on both sides, and are succeeded by the men of the Wycombe Fire Brigade in their blue uniform and jack-boots. From every portion of the neighbourhood, and from many more distant parts, the vast concourse of men and women grouped round the iron railings is collected. On either side grow tall elms, spreading beeches, and many branching oaks. The temptation which these offer to hundreds of lads and men is irresistible. They swarm round the branches; they are perched on the topmost boughs; their heads peep out from many a tuft of delicately green foliage. But not a voice is heard, and the rapt and reverential suspense of soundless expectancy extends its influence everywhere. The procession, which probably numbers more than three hundred persons in its ranks, marches on to no other funeral music than that of the wind as it sighs and rustles through the branches of the trees. There is no check, no sudden quickening of the pace. The deep intonations of the bell correspond almost exactly to each step which is taken; and with this grave harmony of sound and movement the churchyard gate is reached. At the entrance the procession is met by the Rev. Mr. Blagden, with his curate and sexton, and placing themselves at the head, the Vicar commences the impressive Service for the dead, "I am the Resurrection and the Life." The body, and the long line of mourners, move solemnly and slowly to the portals of the church, whose area in a few minutes is filled but is not inconveniently crowded.

The coffin has been deposited on a bier in the chancel, immediately in front of the communion-table. Nothing of the woodwork is visible, and of the magnificent array of wreaths and bouquets which covered it when it left the house not one has been removed or disturbed. At the east end of the bier stand two of Lord Beaconsfield's servants—one of them his confidential valet, who has preceded the coffin, borne by eight labourers on the estate, to the church, holding, as he now holds, the Earl's coronet and the insignia of the Garter on a cushion of deep ruby velvet. In a couple of minutes the sun is hidden by a heavy April cloud, and then, as Mr. Blagden proceeds with the service, the rays burst forth again and flood the whole interior with a sea of liquid gold. Profoundly impressive and profoundly simple the ceremonial is. And its impressiveness is singularly untinged by gloom. The decorations of the church are eloquent of the joyous lessons of Eastertide. Easter mottoes are blazoned on the walls. The altar is adorned with Easter flowers. Not a leaf of cypress or a spray of myrtle is to be seen. We are in the presence of death, but everything seems to tell us that it is death illuminated by the glory of resurrection and life.

Never, it may be safely said, did so small a building

contain so illustrious a company. On the right of the chancel are the Prince of Wales, the Duke of Connaught, Prince Leopold, and others whose position is only less distinguished. In the body of the church are Peers of every degree, the representatives of the greatest Sovereigns in the world, men whose names are part of the history of England. But more interesting and more pathetic than this company of notables is the little group whose members are seated on the left side of the chancel. Here are the men to whom, more than to any others, Lord Beaconsfield was attached, and who tended him during his illness, as they had been indefatigable in their thoughtfulness and care during many years previously. Close to them are two other figures, in whom it is perhaps natural that even more interest should be taken. They are those of Mr. Ralph Disraeli and his son, who is now Lord Beaconsfield's heir, a boy of between thirteen and fourteen years of age, with features which strikingly recall those of his illustrious uncle. The lad submitted yesterday to a trying ordeal, and he bore it with a composure and a gravity which were really remarkable. He was profoundly affected, and his eyes throughout the whole service were full of tears. But there was something of self-reserve and dignity in his grief which was very noticeable. It was not difficult for those who watched him to understand why he should have commended himself to his uncle. "The boy," said Lord Beaconsfield, "has the stuff of a man in him, and I will give him the chance of being one." Of the authenticity of this utterance there is no doubt, and its immediate sequel was that Lord Beaconsfield sent his nephew to Charterhouse, where he now is, and decided that he should be his heir.

When we entered the church the organ was playing, and now, as we begin to leave the church, the same strains are again heard. The coffin is not now carried on the shoulders of the labourers; it is wheeled by them, on the trestles on which it has stood in the chancel, down the aisle, and in this way it is conducted to the grave. Immediately behind the coffin come the mourners and the executors, then the Duke of Connaught and Prince Leopold. After these the Prince of Wales walks by himself. But there is no rigidly set order in the procession, and the whole company walks without any formal marshalling, but in perfect order, to the grave. The vault, as has been already said, is situated at the east end of the church, and a few days ago the entrance to it was completely covered with the soil. The necessary excavations have involved considerable labour, and, as their result, a sloping pathway has been made to the little catacomb. This is covered with a thick woollen carpet, and before the Burial Service in the churchyard begins, the coffin is slowly wheeled to the entrance of the vault. The whole area is utilised for the exhibition of some of the many beautiful floral tributes which have flowed in from all parts of the kingdom. Mrs. Blagden, the wife of the Vicar, has arranged them, and her task is performed with practised skill and admirable taste. Reposing against the headstone, there is placed the magnificent wreath, three feet in diameter, offered by the Junior Carlton Club. This beautiful emblem is composed of white roses and lilac, azaleas, with a central coronet surmounting the letter B, worked in violets, a scroll of violet ribbon bearing the inscription—" From the Junior Carlton Club. In respectful memory." Below is a large book-like box, worked in white camellias, stephanotis, and roses, and filled with violets. Then comes a floral crown, two feet high, formed of the same flowers, which bore the inscription, " A token of remembrance of Benjamin Disraeli, Earl of Beaconsfield, K.G., from one who, though alien in politics, yet not in race, was a fervent admirer of him who 'rose o'er life's tide as lilies o'er the stream,' and earned a Sovereign's gratitude and a nation's love." The juxtaposition of these two offerings suggested the Conservative symbols of Bible and Crown to most of those who inspected them. The Ramsgate Conservative and Constitutional Association sent a coronet of pansies, lilies, camellias, hyacinths, roses, and violets, while kindred bodies all over the country sent wreaths innumerable, and most various and tasteful in design. Many wreaths of single laurel leaves were sent, and to most of the donors of these the same idea had occurred, of emblazoning on the ribbons bearing the inscriptions the Earl's famous Berlin offering "Peace with honour." The grassy slope overlying the vault has been railed off, and built against the wall of the church there are some ornamental stone pilasters and Gothic flutings, in which are inserted three red granite slabs—two small ones, and a large one in between. On the large one is inscribed, in letters of gold, the following:—

"In memory of Mary Anne Disraeli, Viscountess Beaconsfield in her own right, for thirty-three years the wife of the Right Honourable Benjamin Disraeli, Lord of this Manor. Ob. Dec. 15, 1872."

On the slab to the right is the following:—

"In memory of James Disraeli, Esq., one of Her Majesty's Commissioners of Inland Revenue, and the son of Isaac Disraeli, Esq., of Bradenham in this county, author of *Curiosities of Literature*. Ob. Dec. 3, 1868."

On the left-hand slab is the following :—

"In memory of Sarah Brydges Willyams, relict of James Brydges Willyams, of Carnauton, in the county of Cornwall, and Colonel of the Royal Cornish Militia. She died at Torquay, 11th November, 1863, and was buried at her desire in this vault."

## THE FUNERAL.

On the right-hand side of the clergyman were Lords Rowton and Barrington, and just before them Mr. Disraeli and his son. On a line with them were the Prince of Wales and his brothers. The most prominent figure facing them was that of Lord Henry Lennox, and conspicuous among those who were in his immediate neighbourhood were the American Minister, the Marquis of Exeter, Sir Owen Burne, Sir James Brind, and Mr. Gerald Fitzgerald. On the opposite side were the tall figure of Count Münster, Lord Lytton, Sir Frederick Leighton, Sir R. Cross, Sir Stafford Northcote, Sir Charles Whetham, Mr. Raikes, Mr. Ashbury, and many others. Lord Lamington, better known as Mr. Baillie Cochrane, and the original of the "Buckhurst" of *Coningsby*, Lord John Manners, the "Harry Sidney" of the same novel, Lord Salisbury, and most or all of the representatives of latter-day Conservatism, in whom the political influence of Lord Beaconsfield has been most conspicuously manifested, were there too. The silence was intense while the Service was read, and when the words, "Earth to earth, ashes to ashes," were pronounced, the sound of the mould falling against the flowers which strewed the coffin below could distinctly be heard at a distance of many yards. Shortly after four o'clock Mr. Blagden pronounced the blessing, and the company began gradually to disperse. One last tribute to the illustrious dead there yet remained to render. First the mourners, and then all those present in the inclosure, walked down to the vault, and looked for the last time at the coffin containing all that was mortal of Lord Beaconsfield. At a quarter-past five the visitors began to depart. The carriages and cabs came up to the front door of Hughenden Manor, were filled rapidly, and drove off to the station, whence they returned to London.

Shrewsbury, which was represented by Mr. Disraeli in the earlier part of his political career, paid marked tribute to the memory of Lord Beaconsfield. At Canterbury Cathedral the *Dead March* was played on the organ, and the solemn bells in the tower were tolled during the hours of interment. In Liverpool the manifestations of mourning were universal, all the churches ringing muffled peals, and the flags on the public buildings and on the ships in the docks and river being placed at half-mast. The balcony of the Conservative Club was draped in black velvet, with floral wreaths arranged upon it, and the effect was particularly striking and impressive. At the Reform Club the blinds were drawn. Muffled peals were rung at St. Peter's Pro-Cathedral and at the municipal offices. At the monthly meeting of the Chamber of Commerce, the President, Mr. Richard Lowndes, alluded to the universal feeling, quite independent of party, which the death of Lord Beaconsfield had called forth. At Leicester there was a remarkably impressive funeral service during the time of the funeral rites at Hughenden, and at three o'clock a procession of about five hundred leading Conservatives, headed by General Burnaby, made its way to St. Mary's Church, where a vast congregation was assembled, and where a special burial service was read, a suitable funeral sermon being preached by the Rev. Canon Burfield. Coventry has, of course, contributed to the testimony of respect which is now being universally paid to the memory of the deceased statesman, and it is joined in, amongst other places of importance, by Yeovil, South Shields, Newbury, Wakefield, Lichfield, Cardiff, Newport, Leicester, Derby, Chelmsford, Sheffield, and Birmingham. In Maidstone business was totally suspended, and the same may be said, in a more or less degree, for Southend, Stafford, Ludlow, and Dundee. Sympathetic manifestations of feeling were also freely expressed in Exeter, Wolverhampton, Bristol, and Bradford; whilst at Dover, Plymouth, Portsmouth, Gravesend, Greenwich, and the other great naval stations round the coast, the shipping showed its tokens of regret by having the flags half-mast high.

The blinds of the Mansion House were closely drawn from two to four out of respect for the memory of Lord Beaconsfield, with whom the present Lord Mayor sat in the House of Commons, though on different sides, for over ten years, and only official duties in the City prevented his Lordship attending the funeral.

On the following Saturday, April 30th, the Queen, accompanied by the Princess Beatrice, paid a visit to the tomb of the late Earl of Beaconsfield, and the vault, which was again re-opened to receive the royal offerings of affectionate respect, was afterwards finally closed. The visit of Her Majesty was intended to be strictly private, and the secret was most faithfully kept by the few to whom it was confided. On Thursday Lord Rowton was summoned to Windsor, when the Queen intimated her desire to visit Hughenden churchyard and lay on the coffin of the deceased Earl another wreath. The Queen also wished to follow the exact route travelled by Lord Beaconsfield on his last return from Windsor to Hughenden, and to traverse the exact course of the bier on the day of the funeral from the Manor House to the tomb. Lord Rowton communicated Her Majesty's pleasure to the two executors, and on Friday his Lordship and Sir Philip Rose left town for Hughenden, where they were met by Captain Drake, Chief Constable of the county of Bucks, and arrangements were made for securing the desired privacy without exciting public curiosity, which for several days past has been very sensitive in the district in consequence of the trench leading to the vault not having been completely filled in. Rumour accounted for the fact by asserting that an iron door to close the aperture was in course of construction, and when masons were employed on Saturday to re-open the trench, it was generally believed that this was the case. Lord Beaconsfield's last visit to Windsor Castle was on December 8th, and he drove over on his return to Hughenden on the 10th, a distance of about twenty-four miles, calling at Rayners (Sir Philip Rose's estate) on his way home. The route traversed by his Lordship is somewhat circuitous, and as Her Majesty desired to reach Hughenden by the same route, one of Sir Philip's grooms preceded the Royal carriage on Saturday from the entrance to Cleveden (seat of the Duke of Westminster) to Hughenden.

Accompanied by Princess Beatrice, the Dowager Marchioness of Ely (Lady in Waiting), and Lord Charles Fitzroy acting as Equerry, Her Majesty left Windsor in a new carriage drawn by four greys, with postilions and two outriders. Horses were changed at Taplow, and the course from thence pursued was by Dropmore, Hollspur, and along the Oxford road to Lowwater. Turning in at the lower Lodge at Rayners, the Royal party emerged, after a two miles' drive, from the Lodge gates in the rural village of Penn, and thence proceeded by Hazlemere, Deadmandane Bottom, and Crier's Hill to Hughenden Church. The Royal visitors were received by Lord Rowton, who conducted Her Majesty and the Princess into the church, where they were met by the Vicar and his wife. The Queen expressed much admiration at the work of restoration, which has been carried out mainly at the expense of Mr. Seabright, of London, the vicar's father-in-law, and looked with mournful interest on the fast-fading wreaths which fill the seat in the chancel which the late Earl used to occupy. Lord Rowton pointed out where the proposed memorial window would be inserted. Various objects of interest, including the seat formerly occupied by Lord Beaconsfield, were pointed out, and then, after ten minutes' stay within the church, the Royal visitors walked across the greensward to the inclined excavation leading to the opening to the vault. They were followed by the Queen's personal attendant, who carried a beautiful wreath and cross, formed of white camellias and other flowers, exquisitely worked in porcelain, brought in the Royal carriage from Windsor Castle. For a few seconds Her Majesty paused at the head of the incline and stood looking sorrowfully down the sloping path at the open vault. Then, followed by Princess Beatrice, Lord Rowton, the Lady in Waiting, and Lord Charles Fitzroy, Her Majesty walked into the tomb and placed the wreath and cross upon the heap of floral offerings, which completely obscured the lid of Lord Beaconsfield's coffin.

While thus occupied in the vault the Royal

## THE FUNERAL.

visitors were entirely hidden from the gaze of the few assembled spectators, and what really occurred during the few moments the Sovereign stood beside the remains of the late Earl is known only to those who accompanied Her Majesty. When, at last, the sad visit was concluded the Queen and Princess Beatrice emerged slowly from the excavation, and, walking to their carriage, drove from the churchyard, some heavy drops of rain falling as the Royal party proceeded up the steep and winding roadway on the hillside to the small plateau on which the residence of the late Lord Beaconsfield is situated. Entering the private grounds of the Manor House, where the Queen's arrival was heralded by the startled cry of Lord Beaconsfield's favourite peacocks as they strutted about the miniature lawn, Her Majesty and Princess Beatrice alighted at the glass-sheltered piazza, the interior of which is adorned with statuary and foliage plants, and passing into the mansion, engaged for some time in conversation with Lord Rowton. The Royal visitors inspected the Earl of Beaconsfield's study and the other principal apartments, and after a stay of three-quarters of an hour at the house, left Hughenden on their return home. It was half-past five when Her Majesty and Princess Beatrice quitted the ground, the Royal carriage passing down the Park slopes to Wycombe, proceeding thence to Windsor Castle, some heavy showers falling as the Royal party quitted the Hughenden demesne at the close of the visit. Before their departure for London, Lord Rowton and Sir Philip Rose returned to the churchyard, and saw that the masonry work for finally closing the vault was far advanced, Her Majesty having expressed a desire that the vault should not again be opened.

## V.

### LORD BEACONSFIELD'S WILL.

The will of Lord Beaconsfield was read by Mr. P. F. Rose, solicitor, in the saloon at Hughenden Manor immediately after the funeral, and in the presence of the Prince of Wales, the Duke of Connaught, Prince Leopold, and the other distinguished mourners. In this will, which is dated December 16th, 1878, the late Earl bequeaths all his personal estate, including the copyright of his works, to his executors, upon trust that they shall convert it into money, and after the payment of his debts and funeral expenses, apply the residue in the manner subsequently directed. The Manor of Hughenden, with the mansion-house, grounds, and appurtenances, the advowson of the church, and all his landed property in the county of Bucks, are bequeathed to Coningsby Ralph Disraeli, son of Mr. Ralph Disraeli; after Coningsby's decease to his sons, with remainder to the other sons of Mr. R. Disraeli, who may be hereafter born, and failing them, successively to the three daughters of his brother Ralph and their children. Whoever becomes possessed of Hughenden under this will shall take the name of Disraeli only. The trees on the estates are not to be cut down. The mansion and estate may be let during the minority of the heir, which extends to the age of twenty-six years, and the rents applied for the permanent improvement of the property. If they grant leases, the trustees are to reserve "the best yearly rent that can reasonably be gotten without taking any premium." The trustees may sell any portion of the estate, except Hughenden Manor and its grounds, and with the proceeds purchase other freehold or copyhold hereditaments, or discharge any mortgages. A discretion is given them to make a selection from the contents of Hughenden House of articles to be held as heirlooms. The bequest of the papers of the late Earl is in the following words:—

"I give and bequeath to my friend and private secretary, Montagu Corry, Esq., all the letters, papers and documents, whether of a private or of a public character, and whether in print or in manuscript; and also all the manuscript of any writing published or composed by me of which I shall die possessed; and also all the manuscripts and papers of my late father, Isaac Disraeli, Esq., upon the trusts hereinafter declared concerning the same.

"I hereby request the said Montagu Corry, with all convenient speed after my death, to collect, or aid in collecting, the said documents; and I hereby, relying on the discretion of the said Montagu Corry, do authorise and request him to destroy any of the said documents, or any part thereof, as he in the absolute exercise of such discretion shall think ought to be destroyed, and I authorise the said Montagu Corry to keep and deposit all or any of the said documents as he shall think ought not to be destroyed in such place as he shall think fit during such period of time as he shall require to have access to them for the purposes of examination or publication. I give to the said Montagu Corry full discretion with regard to the publication of all or any of such documents, leaving to him to decide as to the time and mode of publication; and as many of the said documents are connected with my official and public life, and contain matters bearing on the character and conduct of contemporary statesmen, and on affairs which it may be of importance to the public interest should not be prematurely or indiscreetly disclosed, I give the above discretion to the said Montagu Corry, in the full assurance that he will scrupulously respect every confidence reposed in me, and will cause or allow nothing to be published calculated to do injury to the public service, or to inflict needless pain on the living or on the families of the dead.

"And I especially and expressly desire and direct that no portion of my correspondence with Her Majesty Queen Victoria shall be published or made known until the said Montagu Corry shall have ascertained and shall have satisfied himself that no objection is entertained to such use of the said correspondence on the part of Her Majesty herself during her life, or after her death on the part of those who may, in the belief of the said Montagu Corry, be likely to be conversant with her wishes and opinions on the subject.

"And I hereby authorise the said Montagu Corry to sell and dispose of the copyright of any of the said documents in the case of their publication, or to make such pecuniary arrangements as to the terms of their publication as he may think fit, and if any less sum than five hundred pounds should, after payment of all expenses of publication, be received by the said Montagu Corry from the publication of any of such documents, I hereby give and bequeath such sum to the said Montagu Corry for his own use; but if any greater sum than the sum of five hundred pounds, after payment of expenses as aforesaid, shall be so received, I desire and direct that the said Montagu Corry shall pay such surplus as soon as the same shall have been actually received and got in by him to the trustees or trustee of this my will, and that the said trustees or trustee of this my will shall apply the same upon the trusts and with and subject to the powers and provisions applicable to moneys arising from sales under the power of sale hereinbefore contained, and investments respecting the same ; but I expressly declare that this proviso shall not be construed to give to any person the right to interfere with any discretion of the said Montagu Corry with regard to the time and mode of publication of the said documents.

" And I hereby authorise the said Montagu Corry to give gratuitous access, whether for historical, literary, or other purposes, to any person or persons to whom in his judgment such access should be given. And with regard to the permanent disposal of the said documents I direct and desire that the said Montagu Corry will, when and so far as is consistent with the due carrying out of the purposes of this my will as to publication and otherwise, deposit the same at my mansion house of Hughenden Manor, and allow the same to go, devolve, and remain as heirlooms, together with my said mansion house, so far as the rules of law and equity will permit, but so, nevertheless, that the same shall not vest absolutely in any person hereby made tenant in tail male, unless such person shall attain the age of twenty-one years ; but on the death of such tenant in tail male under the age of twenty-one years the said documents shall go and devolve and remain as if the same had been freeholds of inheritance and had been devised in strict settlement accordingly.

" And I hereby declare that it shall be lawful for the said Montagu Corry to seal up and keep sealed up all or any of such documents as he shall think proper, and that it shall be lawful at any time for the said Montagu Corry, or for any person bearing an order signed by him, to have access to the said documents, and to make copies of the same, or any part thereof, and for the said Montagu Corry to remove to such place as he shall think proper any of the said documents, and to make copies of the same, or any part thereof ; and for the said Montagu Corry to remove to such place as he shall think proper any of the said documents for such length of time as he may desire, for the purposes of examination or publication. And further, that a list shall be made, subject to revision from time to time, of the said documents not destroyed, and shall be signed by the said Montagu Corry, and by every person for the time being entitled to the use and occupation of my said mansion house, or during the minority of any person who shall be so entitled as aforesaid by the trustees or trustee of this my will, provided always that the said Montagu Corry shall not at any time be responsible for any inadvertent loss or damage which may happen to any of the said documents, but shall not be precluded from interfering for the preservation and protection of the said documents whenever he shall think fit.

"And I hereby declare that if and when the said Montagu Corry shall die or become incapable to act, or be desirous of retiring from the execution of the trusts herein conferred upon him, it shall be lawful for the trustees or trustee of this my will to appoint a successor or successors to the said Montagu Corry in the execution of the said trusts relating to the said documents, and thereupon the execution of the said trusts and all powers and rights hereby conferred on the said Montagu Corry in relation thereto shall devolve on the said successor or successors so appointed as aforesaid, precisely as if he or they had been named in this my will.

"Provided always that all sums of money received by the said Montagu Corry which he would be entitled to keep and retain for his own use under the provisions of this my will shall remain the absolute property of the said Montagu Corry, his executors, administrators, and assigns, and shall not pass to such successor or successors as aforesaid, and such successor or successors shall pay to and account for to the trustees or trustee of this my will all sums of money received by him or them on account of the publication of any of the said documents after payment of all expenses incurred in connection with such publication, and the trustees or trustee of this my will shall apply such sums in the same manner as the money received by them from the said Montagu Corry in respect of the publication of any of the said documents as hereinbefore directed to be applied.

"And I hereby direct and desire that the trustees or trustee of this my will shall collect or aid in collecting the said documents with all convenient speed after my death, and place the same at the disposal of the said Montagu Corry; and I authorise them to pay all the expense of such collection out of my personal estate.

"Provided always, and I hereby declare, that upon every or any appointment of a new trustee of this my will the number of the said trustees may be augmented or reduced, and (in addition to the ordinary powers of indemnity and right to reimbursement by law given to trustees) the trustes, or trustee of this my will shall be at liberty to accept less than a marketable tithe upon the purchase or taking in exchange of any hereditaments, and shall not be answerable for any loss thereby occasioned, nor for any default in title or value of hereditaments purchased or taken in exchange. I hereby appoint the said Sir Nathaniel Mayer de Rothschild and the said Sir Philip Rose executors of this my will."

# VI.

## SUPPLEMENTARY.

THERE can no longer be any doubt as to the place or date of Lord Beaconsfield's birth. It is certain that he was born at 5 or 6, Bloomsbury Square, on December 21, 1804. As regards the place, the following extract from *Bell's Life* of June 19th 1869, is worth reproduction:—

"Sixty years ago, before the police authorities had changed the names of the old thoroughfares, the house, 215, Upper Street, Islington, now divided into two shops, was a well-looking private residence, situate in Trinity Place, its front windows commanding a view of Canonbury fields, its back windows overlooking its own grounds, which were moderately extensive. The then occupier was no less a personage than the elder Disraeli, author of *Curiosities of Literature*, and in that house was born his son, the Hon. Benjamin Disraeli, late Prime Minister of the Crown." Mr. Truefitt, of

No. 5, Bloomsbury Square, however, writes as follows:—"When I took offices here, above five-and-twenty years ago, I was informed by those who had known the house for many years that Benjamin Disraeli was born in this house, and I have never since heard anything to cause me to doubt the believed fact. Yesterday you correctly described the house as at the south-west corner, looking into Hart Street. Mrs. Rust, however, in this morning's paper, has 'assured' you that he was born at No. 6. She is quite right in saying No. 6, but that was the number of this house until the Board of Works took to renumbering houses, and the first one they altered was this, turning it into No. 5, and calling the next house, Mrs. Rust's, No. 6, which till then was 6A or 6½. The rate-books, or any old Directory, will show the correctness of what I state, and I still feel perfectly satisfied that No. 5, Bloomsbury Square (formerly No. 6) was the birthplace of Lord Beaconsfield. When the Disraelis left, it was, after a time, I believe, used as a foreign boarding-house, and then let out into offices, ever since which time, some thirty years ago, it has been a well-known house for gentlemen of my profession, the whole of the sets of rooms, with the exception of the ground floor, being nearly always let to architects."

With reference to the date of the birth, the following is the entry, copied from the baptismal register of St. Andrew's, Holborn:—

"Entry of Baptism, St. Andrew's, Holborn.

"July 31, 1817.—Benjamin, 'sd to be about twelve years old,' son of Isaac and Maria D'Israeli former described as gentleman) residing at King's Rd.—Officiating clergyman, Rev. J. THIMBLEBY."

The subjoined is an exact transcript from the registry of the synagogue in Bevis Marks:—

VESTRY ROOM,
SPANISH AND PORTUGUESE JEWS' SYNAGOGUE,
Bevis Marks, E.C.

| Child's Name. | Father's Name. | Mother's Name. | Surname. | Day in Week of Child's Birth. | Jewish Date. | Christian Era. | Circumcised by | Attested by |
|---|---|---|---|---|---|---|---|---|
| Benjamin. | Isaac. | Maria. | D'Israeli. | Friday. | 19 Tebet, 5565. | 21 December, 1804. | D. A. Lindo, 26 Tebet, 5565. | D. J. De Castro. |

"I hereby certify that the above is a true copy of the entry made in the Registry Book of Births kept at the Spanish and Portuguese Jews' Synagogue, Bevis Marks.

"LONDON, *April* 19, 1881.    E. H. LINDO, *Secretary*."

*The Solicitors' Journal* states that the facts relating to Lord Beaconsfield's connection with the law in early life are these :—

"He was articled to Mr. William Stevens, solicitor, of the firm of Swain, Stevens, Maples, Pearse, and Hunt, of No. 6, Frederick's Place, Old Jewry. The articles of clerkship, which are still preserved by Messrs. Maples, Teesdale, and Co., the successors to the business of the above-mentioned firm, are dated the 10th of November, 1821. Mr. Disraeli, though articled to Mr. Stevens, was exclusively employed in the department of the late Mr. Maples, one of the other partners in the firm, who was an old friend of Mr. Disraeli's father and mother. It was, indeed, through this friendship that Mr. Disraeli came into the office. Mr. Maples always described Mr. Disraeli as being most assiduous in his attention to business, and as showing great ability in its transaction. So marked, indeed, was his talent that Mr. Maples advised Mr. Isaac Disraeli that his son ought to be allowed to go to the bar. This advice was not followed, and Mr. Disraeli remained between three and four years in Messrs. Swain and Co.'s office, but left, we believe, about the beginning of the year 1825."

High Wycombe and its neighbourhood are full of *and* about Lord Beaconsfield. At the White Hart Hotel the landlord exhibits a chair which was made at the time when the late Earl contested High Wycombe, and which was provided by the local chairmakers, who represented the staple industry of the district, for the purpose of chairing the youthful candidate in case he was successful. It is a substantial piece of workmanship, and the story of the use to which it was intended to have been put is indicated by the fact that the colours which the friends of the candidates then bore are worked into it. One little fiction in connection with the late Earl's first candidature has been exposed in the discovery that the large lion which stands on the portico of the Red Lion Hotel, and suggests such stolidity of body and activity of tail, is not the original lion beside which Lord Beaconsfield (then Mr. Disraeli) stood, and on which he leaned when he addressed the electors. The fact is that for two or three years the hotel was without its wooden sign, and the present lion is a modern substitute. Some of the anecdotes told of his Lordship are of the most trivial kind, but the eager way in which they are retailed among the people shows how deep was the impression he made upon his humbler neighbours. It is, however, pleasing to hear the praise that is bestowed upon his memory by those who know how he used frequently to enter the cottages of his tenants, and make practical inquiries as to the sanitary arrangements of their homes. When there were children in the family he would often have them called in, and while they stood in line before him he would put them through a short examination to test their scholastic progress, giving them small rewards in recognition of the ability they displayed.

That the late Earl was held in high esteem among his tenantry is also in many other ways testified. The labourers on his estate speak warmly of him as one who, when they met him sauntering about the sylvan slopes of his little demesne, always had a kind word of inquiry for them and theirs, and who showed a more practical sympathy in winter by judicious gifts of warm clothing and fuel, and who, in conjunction with the Vicar, looked closely after the well-being of three ancient nonagenarians—one ninety-one, another ninety-two, and a third ninety-five—who survive their benefactor, to testify to the healthiness of the Buckinghamshire Downs. Occasionally he extended his walks to the farm-houses of his few tenants, sitting down familiarly, and talking over rural and local matters with them in a simple homely style that won their hearts. There is only one little anecdote told of these periodical excursions concerning a tenant who happened at the time to be suffering from rheumatism. The farm-house was large, and, like many of the homesteads of the district, had brick ground flooring. Speaking more in joke than in earnest, the tenant suggested that this brick flooring had something to do with the malady from which he was suffering, upon which his landlord, taking him *au serieux*, said he could not afford to lose a good tenant for so trifling a matter as that, took his departure, and next day sent a carpenter to substitute a board floor for a brick one. It is also told of him that when a labourer at Hughenden, addressing his Lordship's coachman, and not knowing that his Lordship was in the carriage, asked, "How is the old man to-day?" "I am quite well, thank you," said his Lordship, with a merry twinkle in his eye as he popped his head through the carriage window. Overtaken in his own grounds by two intrusive women, who did not know him, and who asked whether this was "Dizzy's place," he courteously answered their inquiry and directed them to a place from which they might get a good view of the exterior of the house. The women were grievously confused when they afterwards found that they had been addressing his Lordship himself.

# APPENDIX.

# APPENDIX.

On Monday, May 9th, the proposal for erecting a monument to the memory of Lord Beaconsfield in Westminster Abbey was agreed to by both Houses of Parliament. In the House of Lords there was no opposition; in the House of Commons Mr. Labouchere moved an amendment, which was rejected by 380 to 54. The following are the speeches delivered in the House of Lords:—

Earl GRANVILLE.—My Lords, I wish to move the Address of which I have given notice, and which is as follows:—" That an humble Address be presented to her Majesty, praying that her Majesty will give directions that a monument be erected in the collegiate church of St. Peter, Westminster, to the memory of the late Right Hon. the Earl of Beaconsfield, K.G., with an inscription expressive of the high sense entertained by the House of his rare and splendid gifts, and of his devoted labours in Parliament and in great offices of State; and to assure her Majesty that this House will concur in giving effect to her Majesty's most gracious Message." My Lords, very few arguments are required to induce your Lordships to agree to that Motion; and for that reason, and for some others, I shall confine my observations within narrow limits. This is not the time, and I am not the person, to give any biographical sketch of a man so well known as Lord Beaconsfield, and it would still less become me to analyse in any degree his policy or his political action. For me to give my approval of these would give a stamp of insincerity to my remarks which would be displeasing to your Lordships, and which would not be creditable to myself (hear, hear).

My Lords, our long experience of constitutional government has persuaded almost every Englishman that party government is necessary for the well-working of representative institutions, and that party organisation is needful in order to establish a strong and efficient Government under the Constitution (hear, hear). We owe the same experience to other favourable circumstances—that there is no country in which the relations of political opponents are more free from anything like personal bitterness than our own (cheers), or one where there is more readiness on a fitting occasion to drop all party feeling, and to think only of what is good for the dignity of the country (hear, hear). Now, my Lords, I believe it is for the national dignity that Parliament should from time to time, on exceptional occasions, acknowledge the services of statesmen, not thereby giving any general opinion in favour of any particular policy those statesmen may have pursued, but a general recognition of their great abilities having been devoted in eminent situations to the service of the state (hear, hear). My Lords, it is impossible for any one to deny that Lord Beaconsfield played a great part in English history. No one can deny his rare and splendid gifts, and his force of character. No one can deny how long and how continuous have been his services, both with regard to the Crown and Parliament. Lord Beaconsfield achieved by his own strong individuality, without any adventitious circumstances, the great personal success to which he attained. My Lords, I myself, assisted by some of those social advantages which Lord Beaconsfield was without, came into the House of Commons at a very early age, and some six months before Mr. Disraeli took his seat in that assembly. I had thus the opportunity of hearing that speech famous for its failure, although I am convinced that if that speech had been made in a House of Commons which knew him better it would have been received with cheers and sympathetic, instead of derisive, laughter—a speech which, owing to the feeling of his audience, he was obliged to conclude with a sentence somewhat resembling an ejaculation by Mr. Sheridan, which showed the unconquerable confidence which strong men have in their own power. My Lords, the last time that Lord Beaconsfield spoke in this House a speech of an argumentative character was a few weeks ago. I think it was about ten o'clock on the second day of the debate on Afghanistan that Lord Beaconsfield sent me a message saying that he purposed speaking directly. I sent him a strong remonstrance, saying that two peers who had been in office and a third peer, one of the most remarkable speakers in the

House, desired to take part in the debate; but Lord Beaconsfield persisted, and I thought I was justified in making a rather strong complaint of his having done so. I have since learned with regret that Lord Beaconsfield had, just before he received that message from me, swallowed one drug and had inhaled another drug in quantities nicely adapted so as to enable him to speak free from the depression of his complaint during the time that that speech required for delivery. I cannot help thinking that such incidents as these, although not very great in themselves, one at the beginning and the other at the end of a Parliamentary career lasting forty-four years, were proofs of that determination which he possessed and that contempt for obstacles which might have alarmed more weak men (hear, hear). My Lords, I remember another small fact connected with this House which appeared to me indicative of Lord Beaconsfield's self-control and his great patience. I think there are few men coming into the House of Lords as Prime Minister with a great oratorical reputation who would not have shown some impatience for an early opportunity for its display. I daresay your Lordships remember how silent and how reticent Lord Beaconsfield was for two or three months, and it was only when an unfounded charge was made against him that he took the opportunity of making a speech by which he immediately obtained that hold over your Lordships' House which he had so long maintained in another place (hear, hear). My Lords, some men obtain influence over others by possessing in a still stronger degree the merits or the qualities or the faults of those they lead; others produce the same effect by exactly opposite causes. I believe that Lord Beaconsfield, a man himself very free from prejudices, and more or less tolerant of them in others, belonged to the latter class. I have never known any man so complete a master in writing, in speaking, and in conversation, of censure and of eulogy. His long habit of sparkling literary composition, his facility of dealing with metaphor, with antithesis, and even with alliteration, gave him a singular power of coining and applying phrases which caught the popular mind, and which attached praise and blame to the actions of the great parties in the State. My Lords, the noble Earl undoubtedly possessed the power of appealing to the imagination, not only of his countrymen, but of foreigners; and that power was not destroyed even by death. With certain exceptions, Lord Beaconsfield was singularly tolerant with regard to his political opponents, and very appreciative of their merits. I believe no more happy compliment was ever paid to Lord Palmerston and Lord Russell than by Mr. Disraeli in the House of Commons; and I have heard one of Mr. Cobden's dearest friends quote as the most touching speech he ever heard the tribute which Mr. Disraeli paid in the House of Commons to his great and victorious free trade opponent. I myself can boast of having been treated in this House by successive leaders of the great Conservative Party in it with great kindness and great forbearance, but I am bound to say that by none was that great fairness and forbearance more remarkably displayed than by Lord Beaconsfield during the few years that I had the honour of sitting opposite him, and on some previous occasions with regard to Foreign Affairs. My Lords, the noble Duke, speaking on the authority of an intimate friend, told your Lordships how kind and good-natured a man in private life Lord Beaconsfield was. I believe that to be perfectly true, notwithstanding the singular power of destructiveness which he possessed, and sometimes exercised. I remember being told by one to whom the constant devotion of Lord Beaconsfield during his life was one of the characteristic traits of his character, that not only was he a kind and good-natured man, but that he was singularly sensitive to kindness shown to him by others. My Lords, there is one reason why we should pay respect to the memory of Lord Beaconsfield in this House which is not altogether of a disinterested character. The aristocracy of this country, sometimes in praise, sometimes in blame, has been described as proud, powerful, and wealthy. The democratic element, combined with this aristocratic institution, has added to its wealth, to its strength, and possibly to its pride; and I can conceive no brighter, no more brilliant example of the way in which the portals of this Assembly smoothly roll back to admit eminent and distinguished men, and welcome them to the very first ranks in the Assembly that they so enter, than the example of the late Lord Beaconsfield (loud cheers). My Lords, I beg to move the Resolution of which I have given notice.

The Marquess of SALISBURY, who was received with cheers, said :—My Lords, the noble Earl, in the graceful language in which he moved the erection of this last and melancholy tribute to a political opponent, justly said that not only contested questions were in no degree affected by the action that he or your Lordships might take, or the language he used, but also that not many words were needed to commend this Motion to the acceptance of Parliament. In this case, indeed, not many words are needed, because one of the most striking phenomena attending this brilliant and remarkable career has

been the deep interest with which, through his illness and
after his death, his fate was followed not only by his own
friends and adherents, but by men of every class and opinion
in this country, and by men of the greatest influence and
power in other countries also. Whatever else may be said of
the deceased statesman, this, at least, can never be gain-
sayed—that while his memory will ever be associated with
many a controverted issue, the historian must always add
that, when the fierce struggle was over, and the great career
closed, there was no doubt what the verdict was of his
countrymen upon the services he had rendered. This unanimity of opinion with respect to one whose measures were
necessarily much contested will suggest various explanations.
That his friends and colleagues should mourn his loss and
revere his memory is only too natural. I have not the same
title to speak on this subject as many of those beside me, because my close political connection with him was comparatively
recent. But it lasted through anxious and difficult times,
when the character of men may be plainly seen by those
who work with them. And to me, as I believe to all others
who have worked with him, his patience, his gentle-
ness, his unswerving and unselfish loyalty to his colleagues
and fellow-labourers, have made an impression which will
never leave me so long as life endures. But these feelings could only affect a limited circle of his immediate
adherents. The impression which his career and character have made on the vast mass of his countrymen
must be sought elsewhere. To a great extent, no doubt,
it is due to the peculiar character of his genius, to its
varied nature, to the wonderful combination of qualities
which he possessed and which rarely reside in the same brain.
To some extent, also, it is no doubt that the circumstances to
which the noble Earl has so eloquently alluded—that is, the
social difficulties which opposed themselves to his early rise,
and the splendid perseverance by which they were overcome
—impressed his countrymen, who love to see exemplified that
open career to all persons, whatever their initial difficulties
may be, which is one of the characteristics of the institutions
of which they are most proud (hear). They saw in Lord
Beaconsfield's life a proof that whatever difficulties may
attend the beginning of a man's fame, if the genius and
the perseverance are there, the most splendid position and the
widest influence are open to any subject of the Queen. But
there was another cause. Lord Beaconsfield's feelings and
principles with respect to the greatness of his country, more
and more as life went on, made an impression on his country-

men. Zeal for the greatness of England was the passion of his mind (hear, hear). Opinions might and did differ deeply as to the measures and steps by which expression was given to the dominant feelings, and more and more as life drew near its close, as the heat and turmoil of controversy were left behind, as the gratification of every possible ambition negatived the suggestion of any inferior motives, and brought out into greater prominence the purity and strengh of this one intense feeling, the people of this country recognised the force with which this desire dominated his actions, and they repaid it by an affection and reverence which did not depend upon, nor had any concern with, their opinion as to the particular policy pursued. This was the great title to their attachment, namely, that above all things he wished to see England united, powerful, and great. In the questions of interior policy which divided classes he had to consider them, he had to judge them, and to take his course accordingly. It seemed to me that he treated them always as of secondary interest, compared to this one great question — how the country to which he belonged might be made united and strong. The feeling he showed was repaid to him abundantly, and it is because this affection spread itself through all classes, both among those who were his friends and among his opponents, that this vote which has been moved by the noble Earl, and which I have risen to second, is no expression of any party or section of party, is not representative of any opinion upon any controverted question, but is the homage and recognition of a united people to the splendid genius and the magnificent services he rendered (cheers).

The Earl of MALMESBURY.—I should be making a great sacrifice to my own feelings if I did not on this occasion express my opinion, not on the great political powers and talent of Lord Beaconsfield, but as the witness of his private life. My excuse for speaking of him is that I knew him intimately. I knew Lord Beaconsfield before he was a Minister. I was in the first Cabinet in which he sat; I was with him in four Cabinets afterwards, including the last one. With all these opportunities of knowing him, I must say that his was one complete character as far as good nature, amiability, and sincere friendship are concerned. Men might naturally think, when they saw him sitting in the place in which he gained so much honour, with an unmoved countenance, even receiving the thrusts of the greatest gladiators of the day, that he was a man without the common feelings of nature. But that was not the case. I know no man who felt disappointment more, or so much enjoyed triumph. It was his indomitable courrge which enabled him to master his features, as well as supported him through all the difficulties of his career. He had every domestic virtue that I consider a man need have. He was supported by a most amiable and devoted wife, to whom he was equally devoted. I remember when he was at last deprived of her support, he said to me with tears in his eyes, "I hope some of my friends will take notice of me in my great misfortune, for I have now no home. I feel, when I tell my coachman to drive home, that it is a mockery." Her devotion to him is well illustrated by a remarkable story which your Lordships have, no doubt, heard, and which was told me by himself. One day he arrived at the House of Commons, having a very important speech to make. The servant, in closing the door of the carriage, shut in Lady Beaconsfield's fingers. She had the courage not to cry out or make any remark until he was out of sight, lest it should disturb his mind, and have a prejudicial influence on his speech. A very short time before his death he gave an instance of the extraordinary courage and perseverance which existed in his character. I was walking with him one day, and we met an old friend, a gentleman very active formerly in public life, and who had reached the age of eighty-four, still looking, for that age, very young. Lord Beaconsfield said to him, "How is it that you maintain your youthful appearance and health in the way you seem to do?" Our friend answered, "By enjoying all the repose I can." It would be impossible for me to imitate the manner, tone, or gesture with which the late Earl observed, "Ah! repose. Good heavens, repose!" It impressed one more than anything with his invincible determination to continue his labours in the public service of his country. For these reasons, and for the reasons stated by the noble Lords who have proposed and seconded this Vote, it is our duty and pleasure to raise a monument to this great Englishman (hear, hear).

The Motion was then agreed to.

In the House of Commons Mr. Gladstone and Sir Stafford Northcote spoke as follows:—

Mr. GLADSTONE having moved that the Speaker leave the Chair, the motion was agreed to, and the House went into Committee on the monument in Westminster Abbey to the late Earl of Beaconsfield.

Mr. GLADSTONE, amid loud Ministerial cheers, then rose to move the following resolution:—" That an humble Address he presented to her Majesty, praying that her Majesty will give directions that a monument be erected in the Collegiate Church of St. Peter, Westminster, to the memory of the late Right Hon. Earl of Beaconsfield, with an inscription expressive of the high sense entertained by the House of his rare and splendid gifts, and of his devoted labours in Parliament and in great offices of State, and to assure her Majesty that this House will make good the expenses attending the same." The right hon. gentleman said,—Sir, considering the notice of amendment that appears in conjunction with my own upon the paper, it would perhaps be too sanguine were I to express even the faintest hope that this motion may receive the unanimous assent of the Committee. But, sir, while I do not venture to express that hope, I do entertain a very earnest hope, I would even say I offer a most earnest entreaty, that it may not be made a subject of lengthened or contentious argument (cheers). I say that in the condition of one especially bound to consider what is for the dignity of the House, but I say it also in the character of an old and keen opponent of Lord Beaconsfield; and nothing would be so painful to me—except, indeed, the rejection of the vote, which I think impossible—as that its grace should be entirely marred by its being a subject of angry discussion (hear, hear). It has not been unnatural that on a subject of this kind, exciting so much and so varied public interest, criticism should have been busy; and on that criticism, both in respect of what has been done, and in respect of what has not been done, I will simply say that my object has been the fulfilment of my duty, and that fulfilment of my duty has appeared to lie in a careful consideration of the rules and precedents applicable to the case. I think that those precedents ought to be liberally interpreted, but for my own part, in all these monumental and complimentary matters, I have great jealousy of adding to them. There is a temptation under the influence of feeling to make these additions, and every addition made on a particular occasion becomes an embarrassment in the next. I will simply say, not that I have interpreted the precedents aright—I will not assume that—but I have endeavoured strictly and carefully to make them my guide. Every one will feel that this is not an occasion to attempt an historical portrait of Lord Beaconsfield; neither is it the occasion to attempt, especially on this side of the House, or from no side of the House, I will venture to say, is it the occasion to attempt a political eulogy of Lord Beaconsfield. It would be mistaking the purpose for which we are met. I would go a little further, and admit

that the position of the House is, in some respects, and in
part, peculiar. I do not know that it has ever happened that
a Parliament in sharper antagonism to the policy of a particular Minister has been called upon to accept a proposition of
this kind with respect to that Minister whose policy it had
opposed; but at the same time, though there is no case
exactly analogous to this, yet there are cases which make a
material approximation to it in those very respects. When
Lord Russell proposed, in 1850, in a speech of great taste,
a monument to the memory of Sir Robert Peel, he very
naturally looked back, not merely to the crisis of the anti-
corn-law movement, which had brought them together, but
to the long struggles of thirty years; and Lord Russell
said, in very becoming language, "I will not enter into the
nature of the measures with which his name is associated;" and again, "this is not the time to consider
particular opinions or particular measures." But he also
quoted an earlier case, in which it happened that Colonel
Barré proposed a public monument to Lord Chatham, with
whom he himself, no very long time before, had been in the
sharpest antagonism, so that although the features of this
case are marked features, yet we are not without guidance
from the proceedings of those who have gone before. But
this I will venture to say, that this is an occasion on which I
should affirm that a majority of this side of the House ought
to be on their guard against giving way to our own narrower
political sympathies (Ministerial cheers). It would be better
that propositions of this kind were to be altogether abandoned
and forgotten than that they should degenerate into occasions
for issuing a manifesto of political alliances or ordinary par-
tisanships (hear, hear). If I am asked why, endeavouring
to look without fear or favour at this case upon its merits and
upon nothing else, and desirous of speaking the truth without
restraint, but without exaggeration—why I venture to recommend this proposition to the House, why I think that the
same reasons which have led the House to give, in the case
of other Prime Ministers of this country, a testimony such
as I now invite to the memory of Lord Beaconsfield, I say
that in my judgment we have to look to two questions, and
to two questions only, and these are, whether the tribute it is
proposed to pay is proposed to be paid to one who in the first
place has sustained a great historic part and done great deeds,
written on the page of Parliamentary and national history;
and the other, whether these deeds have been done with the
full authority of the constituted organs of the nation and of
the nation itself. I think that an impartial regard to what

has happened will satisfy the House that upon neither of
these points is there the smallest room for doubt. It
may seem to be a sharp mental transition for us to make
when we pass from the balance of political opinion which
now prevails in this House to the balance of opinion which
subsisted here two, three, or four years ago. But it is
right, it is just, it is necessary, that we should reflect that
what was done by the late Parliament, what was done by the
late Ministry, what was done, above all, by Lord Beaconsfield, as the official head and as the guiding spirit of the
whole Ministry, was done under precisely the same Constitutional title and exactly the same charter and authority as that
under which we now claim to act (Ministerial cheers).
Therefore I cast behind me for a moment the question of
what I approve and what I disapprove, what I rejoice at and
what I regret. We are here to act on the part of the nation,
and to maintain that description of action which is suitable to
and which is required by a nation's continuous life. The
career of Lord Beaconsfield is, in many respects, the most
remarkable one in Parliamentary history. For my own part,
I know but one that can fairly be compared to it in regard to
the emotion of surprise, and when viewed as a whole, an
emotion, I might almost say, of wonder, and that is the career,
and especially the earlier career, of Mr. Pitt. Lord Beaconsfield's name is associated with great Constitutional changes—
at least with one great Constitutional change, in regard to
which I think it will ever be admitted, at least I never can
scruple to admit, that its arrival was accelerated by his personal act (hear, hear). I will not dwell upon that, but I
will simply mention the close association of his name with
that important change in the principle of the Parliamentary
franchise. It is also associated with great European transactions and great European arrangements. I feel myself in
the position, not necessarily of a friend and admirer, who
looks with sympathy at the character and action of Lord
Beaconsfield, but I look at the magnitude of the part which
he played on behalf of his country, and I say that one who
was his political friend might fairly have said of him when
he came back from Berlin—

> "Aspice, ut insignis spoliis Marcellus opimis
> Ingreditur, victorque viros supereminet omnes."

(Cheers.) My duty is to look at these things in the magnitude
of their national and historical character, and it is in so looking at them that I have no doubt that the man who for seven
years sustained the office of Prime Minister, the man who for

nearly thirty years led, either in one House or in both, a great party of this country, and the man who had so intertwined himself in the interest of the general heart, as was shown upon the occasion of his illness, is a man in whom those features meet which justify me in asking for this vote. I have said that, in my opinion, the magnitude of the part which he played, and the authority on which it was played, are the only matters to which we can look. I would press this point especially, for it is one many of us might forget or only feebly or ineffectually remember—namely, that he acted with the same authority as that which we claim for ourselves. The same Constitution, the same popular liberties, the same franchises, the same principle of the prevalence of the majority placed him, first in this House and then in the House of Lords, to give effect to the policy which he believed to be for the benefit of his country (cheers), and which have now placed other men in his position to give effect to what they, with equal sincerity, desire to recommend to Parliament. I think that that somewhat dry portion of my duty which I have now performed in directing attention to those two points which I deem to contain the whole estimate of the case is concluded. As I have said, I will not attempt to give anything like a historial portrait. It would not be fair or frank, even if it were appropriate in point of time, that I who have been separated from Lord Beaconsfield by longer and larger differences than perhaps ever separated any two persons brought into constant contact in the transaction of public business—it would not be fair to him, it would not be fair to his friends, that I should endeavour to draw a picture of him which must be more faintly coloured, and I must add, which must be differently coloured, if executed by my hand than that which they could fairly claim (hear, hear). But yet, sir, I will allow myself some satisfaction in dwelling on matters upon which I feel it is pleasurable to myself, and on which I also think it is useful for us all to dwell. There were certain great qualities of the deceased statesman on which I think it right to touch. His extraordinary intellectual powers are as well understood by others as by me, and they are not proper subjects for our present commendation. But there were other great qualities—qualities not merely intellectual in the sense of being dissociated from conduct, but qualities immediately connected with conduct, with regard to which I should say, were I a younger man, that I should like to stamp the recollection of them on myself for my own future guidance, and with regard to which I will confidently say to those who are younger than myself that I would strongly recommend them for notice and imitation (cheers). They were qualities not only written in a marked manner on his career, but possessed by him in a degree undoubtedly extraordinary. I speak, for example, of such as these—his strength of will; his long-sighted persistency of purpose, reaching from the first entrance on the avenue of life to its very close; his remarkable powers of self-government; and last, but not least, of all, his great Parliamentary courage, a quality in which I, who have been associated in the course of my life with some scores of Ministers, have never known but two whom I could pronounce to be his equal. There were some other points in his character upon which I cannot refrain from saying one word. I wish to express the admiration I have always felt for his strong sympathy with his race, for the sake of which he was always ready to risk popularity and influence (cheers). A like sentiment I feel towards the strength of his sympathy with that brotherhood to which he thought, and justly thought, he was entitled to belong—the brotherhood of men of letters. With struggling genius his sympathy was ever ready, and in a book of the greatest interest, the *Autobiography* of Mr. Thomas Cooper, within the last few days I have read how, in the year 1844, when Lord Beaconsfield's character with his party, and his influence with his party, were not yet established, and when Mr. Cooper appeared before him in the character of a struggling literary man, who was also a Chartist, Mr. Disraeli met him with the most generous and active sympathy (cheers). There was a feeling, Sir, lying yet nearer the very centre of his existence which, though a domestic feeling, may now without indelicacy be referred to—his profound, his devoted, tender, and grateful affection for his wife (cheers), which, if as may be the case—I know not whether it be so or not—has deprived him of the honour of public obsequies, has nevertheless left for him a more permanent title as one who knew, even amidst the calls and temptations of political life, what was due to the sanctity and strength of domestic affection, and which made himself an example in that respect to the country in which he lived (cheers). I have expressed the hope that the debate may not be a lengthened debate, and I wish that my own contribution to it should be confined within the limits of necessity. I believe that if the House has been kind enough to listen to the few words which I have used I have set before them all that is necessary, perhaps all that is warrantable, for me to say. There is, however, one slighter matter on which I desire to give myself the satisfaction of a brief reference to Lord Beaconsfield. The feeling I am about to express is not a novel feeling. It is one which for many long years on the occasions of private life has been made known to me by my friends. There is much error and misapprehension abroad as to the personal sentiments that prevail between men who are divided in politics (cheers). Their words must necessarily from time to time be sharp; their judgments may occasionally, may warrantably, may necessarily be severe; but the general idea of persons less informed than those within the Parliamentary circle is that they are actuated towards one another by sentiments of intense antipathy or hatred. I wish to take this occasion, with the permission of the House—if for a moment I may degenerate into egoism upon a subject much too high for it— I wish to record in this place and at this hour my firm conviction that in all the judgments ever delivered by the late Lord Beaconsfield on myself, he was never actuated by sentiments of personal antipathy (cheers). It is a pleasure to me to make that acknowledgment. It is not new, although it is one that could hardly with propriety be made on an earlier occasion. I am sure the House will excuse me for having obtruded it now (cheers). Upon calling the attention of the House to the fact that what we have to look at to-night is the greatness of the man, the greatness of the offices sustained by him, the greatness of the part he played, the greatness of the transactions associated with his name, and finally the full and undisputed Constitutional authority which he possessed for those actions, whether they were according to our sense and taste or not—that full plenary Constitutional power which he possessed to authorise beforehand and to sanction afterwards what he did. These are the essential considerations that ought to guide us; and I feel convinced —unless it be my own grievous fault, and if so I can but regret it—that I have said enough to show the Committee that they will do well and wisely to accept in a kindly spirit the Motion which I have now the honour to submit on behalf of a public monument to Lord Beaconsfield (cheers).

Sir S. NORTHCOTE.—In rising to second the Motion just proposed I shall say but a very few words, because I am sure I shall best fulfil the wishes of the House, and best respond to the spirit in which the Motion has been made, if I abstain from anything that can in the slightest degree derogate from the tone which has been given to the discussion by the speech of the right hon. gentleman. If I could contemplate for a moment that this motion should not meet with the general—

R

let me say I hope the unanimous, acceptance of the Committee, in a spirit and manner satisfactory to those who long to see this mark of honour paid to one whom they love, we should at least feel that a monument of a higher character than any that could be carved in stone and marble has been already erected to Lord Beaconsfield in the speech to which we have just listened (cheers). Sir, that speech has been nobly expressed, and, still more, it has been nobly conceived. I venture to say that in this tribute paid to the memory of a sharp political opponent by one who has been engaged for so many years in the severest of political contests, we have a record which will be not merely for the honour of the speaker, not merely for the honour of whom the words were spoken, but for the honour of the British House of Commons (cheers). It is a true key that has been struck in our political life and contest. Taking up the last words of the Prime Minister, and speaking as one who had a large share of the private confidence and intimacy of our distinguished friend—who has sat by his side for many years in the midst of contests, and who had also the privilege of enjoying his confidence in quiet and retired moments—I can entirely, and from the bottom of my heart, confirm the saying of the Prime Minister that in all those contests, ready as he always was to enter into the battle—sharp as his words were in the course of action—there was nothing in his mind or spirit that was unworthy of a generous antagonist (cheers). No personal feeling was allowed to warp a sentiment of admiration for his chief political rival (hear, hear). I feel that this is not a moment in which I could appropriately address the Committee as I could wish to do. It is not a moment for the indulgence of private feeling. Although we have been connected together on occasions of contest and public debate, yet there is much beside and behind that to those who were intimate with Lord Beaconsfield it would be painful to attempt to parade. There was much in him to love ; there was much in his sympathy and readiness at all times to give advice, to enter into every difficulty, however trifling it might be, to encourage when encouragement was wanted, to warn and assist where he thought warning and assistance necessary, which greatly endeared him to those who knew him (cheers). It would be less appropriate were I to attempt to enter at such a moment as this —it would be an outrage on the House were I to draw anything like a political character which would be in the nature of a political eulogium (hear, hear). I distinguish such occasions as those which are characteristic of the British House of Commons and the British nation from those eulogiums

which are passed sometimes in other countries at the funerals
of men who have borne a distinguished part in party war-
fare—occasions which are sometimes used for the purpose of
glorifying and promoting the objects of political parties. We
have nothing of that sort here; we are here engaged for a
a moment, pausing in the midst of our political strife, in
placing a wreath on the bier of a champion who has fallen
amongst us, and who we all, on both sides, are prepared to
honour. I could quite understand that if there was anything
in the proposal that seemed to pledge the House and the
country to an approval of the particular policy of Lord
Beaconsfield, there would be difficulties raised in many
quarters to paying a tribute that might be misunderstood.
But such is not the case. We are now doing honour to
a man whose rare gifts we have all admired, and which
have been acknowledged by all those who have had any
opportunity of witnessing their display. We are doing
honour to a man who never quailed before danger, who
never allowed himself to be disheartened by defeat or
discouraged by difficulty, who always kept a high standard
before him—whether it approved itself to all men or not
I will not say—and who never, under any difficulties or
circumstances, lost sight of or shrank from the standard
he so displayed. When he came to the post of dignity to
which he had so fairly fought his way against the greatest
obstacles and discouragements, he commanded not only the
respect of the people of this country, but the respect of
those among whom he sat and took his place as the representative of Britain in the affairs of foreign countries.
We have been reminded that the public honours which it was
desired to be conferred upon him at his funeral were ex-
changed for a funeral of a more private character, that was
not only in accordance with his written directions, but with
the whole spirit of his life. He was one who above all
things rejoiced in that retirement of which he was allowed to
enjoy so small a portion, and his heart was in the home and
sepulchre in which his body is now placed (hear, hear). Although his funeral was private, although there was nothing
in the nature of invitation to the nation to it, yet that England was there—that the occasion was one in which the hearts
of the people, whatever may have been their rank or distinction, were turned to Hughenden, there was no doubt. Whether
or not you have a memorial erected to him in this or any other
place of public notoriety, the name and fame of him whom
we have lost is secure in the memories of Englishmen, and
will never perish (cheers).

On these speeches in both Houses of Parliament *The Standard* published the next day this leading article:—

The English Parliament has rarely been engaged in a labour more deserving of its high character than that which occupied both Houses for a brief interval on their assembly yesterday. The proposal that a Monument should be erected to the late Lord Beaconsfield in Westminster Abbey, at the public expense, was introduced in the Lords by Earl Granville, and in the Commons by the Prime Minister, in speeches which, differing from each other as they did in every other respect, resembled each other in a striking manner in the elevated tone and the discriminating taste by which both were marked. Lord Granville, perhaps, was never heard to greater advantage than while dwelling on the familiar characteristics of the great Statesman whom only a few weeks ago he was opposing with all the vigour of English Parliamentary life. There is no greater art in oratory than the apt introduction of personal reminiscences, and frequently as the English people have read of the dramatic incident of the first speech delivered by Lord Beaconsfield in the House of Commons forty-four years ago, Lord Granville contrived to confer on it a novel interest, and almost a novel character, by the skilful manner in which he recalled the fact that he himself formed part of the audience on that famous occasion. We hear much in these days of the degeneracy of Parliamentary manners; but it may be doubted if even the present House of Commons would, under the utmost provocation, treat its most unpopular member with the discourtesy and the injustice Lord Granville admits were inflicted upon Mr. Disraeli when he first sought to gain the ear

of the Legislature. The allusion to the latest serious
effort of Lord Beaconsfield to address the House of
Lords, and to the physical measures he found it
necessary to adopt in order to secure that effort
against failure, was skilfully associated with the indomitable self-confidence of his earliest Parliamentary
experiences, and Lord Granville was thereby enabled
to point his moral with telling effect, and to pronounce
a eulogium as just as it was generous upon the unconquerable will which from first to last triumphed
over all obstacles. It is easier to extol a foe than
a friend, and panegyric is necessarily more interesting
when it proceeds from an opponent than from an
avowed ally. Thus Lord Salisbury was at some dis-
advantage when he rose, in his new character of
Leader of the Conservative Party in the House of
Lords, to second the proposal of the Government.
Nevertheless, more difficult as was his task, he acquitted himself of it in a manner worthy of the
occasion and of the assembly he was addressing.
Eschewing, with instinctive tact, any laudation of the
policy of his departed chief, Lord Salisbury brought
out into salient relief the important fact that the
consuming passion of Lord Beaconsfield's political
life was anxiety for the greatness and the glory of
England. Whilst accepting the assertion to the full,
we may add that this passion was rather the growth
of life and experience than a strong innate sentiment.
But no one who watched Lord Beaconsfield closely,
or who enjoyed his political intimacy, could fail to
remark that of late years, this zeal for the greatness
of the English Empire assumed ever larger dimensions,
until in the last resort what he deemed the humilia-
tion of his country became to him a deep personal
sorrow. No one will complain that the Earl of
Malmesbury, so long associated in the Public Service
with the deceased Statesman, should add his personal

testimony to the engaging qualities of his colleague and friend, or supplement the panegyric upon his public talents with a graceful reference to his private virtues and his domestic tenderness. Perhaps the House of Lords would have been willing to prolong the Debate, had its prolongation been caused by a few words from Lord Derby. This hope was formed, but it was not gratified.

Public curiosity was, perhaps, attracted yesterday more to the Lower than the Upper House, for it was known that Mr. Gladstone had returned to town, and would himself perform the task that had devolved upon Lord Granville in the other Chamber. The Prime Minister acquitted himself of a difficult duty with a grace that must baffle the most captious of his critics. He was not effusive; he would have sinned against good taste, had such been his tone. But his eulogium was dignified and ungrudging; and Sir Stafford Northcote accurately reflected its character when he observed that it was nobly conceived and nobly expressed. English public life demands some hard hitting from its political athletes; and just as Lord Granville observed that Lord Beaconsfield was a master equally of censure and of praise, so the Prime Minister showed last night that he can appreciate great qualities as freely as he can denounce what he conceives to be a vicious policy. Alone of the speakers in both Houses, Mr. Gladstone placed the proposal to erect a National Monument to Lord Beaconsfield on a proper and unanswerable footing. It is strange that Mr. Labouchere should not have felt that his objections were answered in anticipation by his own Leader. The only approach to argument to be found in the honourable member's speech was the contention that splendid gifts are imperious, and to be deprecated when they are employed to the detriment of the State. As Mr. Gladstone pointed out with admirable force, whether the gifts of any particular Statesman are employed to the public advantage is a matter of opinion ; and the opinion of what is called the Nation is a fluctuating one. Three years ago the Nation would almost to a certainty have pronounced overwhelmingly in Lord Beaconsfield's favour. Who shall say what opinion, three years hence, it may record, or have recorded, of the policy of those who superseded him? It is enough to point out, as the Prime Minister says, that he did great things, and did them under the same constitutional title, the same charter and authority which can be pleaded by any Statesman, dead or living, for his public measures and public policy. A defence of Lord Beaconsfield so complete and so conclusive from the mouth of Mr. Gladstone naturally left Sir Stafford Northcote little to say, save to echo the praises he had listened to, and endorse the reasoning in which he had been anticipated. Like Lord Salisbury, Sir Stafford Northcote had to bewail the loss of a friend as well as to do justice to the memory of a Statesman ; and the voice of private frendship is apt to quiver and wax inarticulate when it ventures upon notes of public appreciation.

The country has no reason to be dissatisfied with the issue of a proposal which at one time threatened to engender acrimony and scandal. The faint and futile opposition with which it has been encountered by persons to whom we are quite willing to ascribe conscientious motives, while reproaching them with somewhat questionable taste and wholly irrelevant argument, has only served to bring into bolder outline the general unanimity of sentiment with which the suggestion of the Government has been met. In spite of his faults, the English people are proud of Lord Beaconsfield. They will cherish his memory because they feel that he added lustre to the country he served, and possessed those elements of grandeur in his character which redeem public life from interested motives and unseemly rivalries. Upon his opponents, as well as upon his colleagues, while he lived, he reflected something of the lustre of his own distinction, and it is possible that men who seemed great so long as they were his rivals will lose something of their eminence now that he is gone. As the Prime Minister observed yesterday, the interest and attraction of Lord Beaconsfield's career are unmatched in our Parliamentary annals, even by the younger Pitt. But mere romantic or dramatic effect does not suffice to collect a nation at the grave of a deceased Statesman. No doubt Lord Beaconsfield captivated the world by the brilliancy of his wit. But he secured the lasting approval of its judgment by the sobriety of his understanding. He was at once an original and practical Statesman. His originality cannot easily be imitated. But his good sense and his patriotic resolution may be studied with effect.

THE END.

**SPENSER.** By the Very Rev. the DEAN OF ST. PAUL'S. Crown 8vo. 2s. 6d.

"Dr. Church is master of his subject, and writes always with good taste."—*Academy.*

**THACKERAY.** By ANTHONY TROLLOPE. Crown 8vo. 2s. 6d.

"Mr. Trollope's sketch is excellently adapted to fulfil the purpose of the series in which it appears."—*Athenæum.*

**BURKE.** By JOHN MORLEY. Crown 8vo. 2s. 6d

"It is no disparagement to the literary studies already published in this admirable series, to say that none of them have surpassed, while few have equalled, this volume on Burke."—*British Quarterly Review.*

**MILTON.** By MARK PATTISON. Crown 8vo. 2s. 6d.

"The writer knows the times and the man, and of both he has written with singular force and discrimination."—*Spectator.*

**HAWTHORNE.** By HENRY JAMES, Junr. Crown 8vo. 2s. 6d.

"Probably no one living could have done so good a book on Hawthorne as Mr. James has done."—*Saturday Review.*

**SOUTHEY.** By Professor DOWDEN. Crown 8vo. 2s. 6d.

"A truly scholarly and delightful monograph of a great writer, who has been of late years undeservedly neglected."—*Examiner.*

**CHAUCER.** By Professor A. W. WARD. Crown 8vo. 2s. 6d.

"An enjoyable and excellent little book is this of Professor Ward's. Far away the best connected account of Chaucer and his work to be found in English."—*Academy.*

**BUNYAN.** By JAMES A. FROUDE. Crown 8vo. 2s. 6d.

"The life and character of Bunyan stand out in bold relief, and for the first time the author of the 'Pilgrim's Progress' is pourtrayed as he really existed."—*Westminster Review.*

**POPE.** By LESLIE STEPHEN. Crown 8vo. 2s. 6d.

"The sketch of Pope's life which Mr. Leslie Stephen has written is interesting throughout. . . . A work which one can only lay down with a wish to have a good deal more on the same subject from the same hand."
—*Academy*.

**BYRON.** By Professor NICHOL. Crown 8vo. 2s. 6d.

"Decidedly one of the most careful and valuable of the whole series. When a book is as good as Professor Nichol's, there is little to be said about it, except to recommend it as widely as may be."—*Athenæum*.

**COWPER.** By GOLDWIN SMITH. Crown 8vo. 2s. 6d.

"Mr. Goldwin Smith has sketched in a few decisive touches the genius of the poet and the weakness of the man."—*Daily News*.

**LOCKE.** By Professor FOWLER. Crown 8vo. 2s. 6d.

"In the case of Locke's biographer, we venture to say that Mr. Morley has been exceptionally fortunate. A pen more competent than Professor Fowler's for this particular work might have been sought, and sought in vain."—*Examiner*.

**WORDSWORTH.** By F. W. H. MYERS. Crown 8vo. 2s. 6d.

"Mr. Myers gives us a picture of the man and an estimate of his work which is certainly not inferior to anything that has preceded it. Possibly the best chapter in the book—every chapter is excellent—is that on Natural Religion."—*Academy*.

**DRYDEN.** By GEORGE SAINTSBURY. Crown 8vo. 2s. 6d.

### IN PREPARATION.

**SWIFT.** By JOHN MORLEY.
**ADAM SMITH.** By LEONARD H. COURTNEY, M.P.
**BENTLEY.** By Professor R. C. JEBB.
**LANDOR.** By Professor SIDNEY COLVIN.
**DICKENS.** By Professor A. W. WARD.
**DE QUINCEY.** By Professor MASSON.
**BERKELEY.** By Professor HUXLEY.
**CHARLES LAMB.** By Rev. ALFRED AINGER.
**STERNE.** By H. D. TRAILL.

*Others will follow.*

MACMILLAN & CO., LONDON.

# MESSRS. MACMILLAN & CO.'S PUBLICATIONS.

## NEW BOOKS ON IRELAND.

**EDMUND BURKE'S LETTERS AND PAPERS ON IRISH AFFAIRS.** Edited, with a Preface, by MATTHEW ARNOLD. Crown 8vo. [*Immediately.*

*\** Mr. GLADSTONE *in his speech on the Irish Land Bill, April 7, referred to Professor Richey's book as "a very able, although concise work."*

**THE IRISH LAND LAWS.** By ALEXANDER G. RICHEY, Q.C., LL.D., Deputy Regius Professor of Feudal and English Law in the University of Dublin. Crown 8vo. 3s. 6d.

**NEW VIEWS ON IRELAND, OR IRISH LAND GRIEVANCES AND REMEDIES.** By CHARLES RUSSELL, Q.C., M.P. Crown 8vo, cloth. 2s. 6d.

"They should be studied by every one who desires to understand the existing crisis in Ireland."—SPECTATOR.

**THE LIFE'S WORK IN IRELAND OF A LANDLORD WHO TRIED TO DO HIS DUTY.** By W. BEN JONES, of Lisselan. Crown 8vo. 6s.

"Mr. Bence Jones, every one must own, has a fair claim to be heard, and no one can be in a position properly to discuss Irish affairs till he has read his really valuable book."—LITERARY WORLD.

**DISTURBED IRELAND**, being Letters written during the Winter of 1880—81. By BERNARD H. BECKER, Special Commissioner of the *Daily News*. With Route Maps. Crown 8vo. 6s.

"Nothing better in the way of special correspondence has perhaps ever been seen, and the book will be invaluable to every M.P. wishing to understand the burning question of the time."—THE WORLD.

---

**THE IRISH CRISIS**, being a Narrative of the Measures for the Relief of the Distress caused by the Great Irish Famine of 1846—47. By Sir CHARLES TREVELYAN, Bart., K.C.B. 8vo. Price 2s. 6d.

**THE LAND-WAR IN IRELAND**: A HISTORY FOR THE TIMES. By JAMES GODKIN, Author of "Ireland and Her Churches," late Irish Correspondent of the *Times*. Demy 8vo. 12s.

MACMILLAN & CO., LONDON.

# MESSRS. MACMILLAN & CO.'S PUBLICATIONS.

*BY THE RIGHT HON. HENRY FAWCETT, M.P.*

THE ECONOMIC POSITION OF THE BRITISH LABOURER. Extra fcap. 8vo. 5s.

SPEECHES ON SOME CURRENT POLITICAL QUESTIONS. 8vo. 10s. 6d.

CONTENTS:—Indian Finance—The Birmingham League—Nine Hours Bill—Election Expenses—Women's Suffrage—Household Suffrage in Counties—Irish University Education, &c.

FREE TRADE and PROTECTION. An Inquiry into the Causes which have retarded the general adoption of Free Trade since its Introduction into England. Third Edition. 8vo. 7s. 6d.

*BY W. T. THORNTON, C.B.,*

LATE SECRETARY FOR PUBLIC WORKS IN THE INDIA OFFICE.

A PLEA for PEASANT PROPRIETORS, with the Outlines of a Plan for their Establishment in Ireland. New Edition. Crown 8vo. 7s. 6d.

ON LABOUR; its Wrongful Claims and Rightful Dues, Actual Present and Possible Future. Second Edition, revised, 8vo. 14s.

---

The LAND QUESTION, with Particular Reference to England and Scotland. By JOHN MACDONELL, Barrister-at-Law. 8vo. 10s. 6d.

LAWRENCE BLOOMFIELD in IRELAND; or, The New Landlord. Cheaper Issue, with New Preface. By WILLIAM ALLINGHAM. Fcap. 8vo. 4s. 6d.

COMMENTARIES on the LIBERTY of the SUBJECT, and the LAWS of ENGLAND RELATING to the SECURITY of the PERSON. By JAMES PATERSON, Barrister-at-Law. Cheaper Issue. Two vols. Crown 8vo. 21s.

The LIBERTY of the PRESS, SPEECH, and PUBLIC WORSHIP. Being Commentaries on the Liberty of the Subject and the Laws of England. By JAMES PATERSON, Barrister-at-Law. Crown 8vo. 12s.

MACMILLAN AND CO., LONDON.

# MESSRS. MACMILLAN & CO.'S PUBLICATIONS.

**BLACKS, BOERS, AND BRITISH: a Three-Cornered Problem.** By F. R. STATHAM. Crown 8vo. 6s.

"His lively book.... It is a picture of South Africa itself.... His book shows a complete grasp of the subject and great power of presentation and description."—DAILY NEWS.

## BY THE RIGHT HON. JOHN BRIGHT, M.P.

**SPEECHES ON QUESTIONS OF PUBLIC POLICY.** Edited by Professor THOROLD ROGERS, M.P. Author's Popular Edition. Globe 8vo. 3s. 6d.

"Mr. Bright's speeches will always deserve to be studied, as an apprenticeship to popular and parliamentary oratory; they will form materials for the history of our time, and many brilliant passages, perhaps some entire speeches, will really become a part of the living literature of England."—DAILY NEWS.

**LIBRARY EDITION.** Two Vols. 8vo. With Portrait. 25s.

**PUBLIC ADDRESSES.** Edited by J. THOROLD ROGERS, M.P. 8vo. 14s.

**RICHARD COBDEN'S SPEECHES ON QUESTIONS OF PUBLIC POLICY.** Edited by the Right Hon. JOHN BRIGHT, M.P., and JAMES E. THOROLD ROGERS, M.P. Extra fcap. 8vo. 3s. 6d.

**PRACTICAL POLITICS.**—ISSUED BY THE NATIONAL LIBERAL FEDERATION:—
I. THE TENANT FARMER: Land Laws and Landlords. By JAMES HOWARD. 8vo. 1s.
II. FOREIGN POLICY. By Right Hon. M. E. GRANT DUFF, M.P. 8vo. 1s.
III. FREEDOM OF LAND. By G. SHAW LEFEVRE, M.P. 8vo. 2s. 6d.
IV. BRITISH COLONIAL POLICY. By SIR DAVID WEDDERBURN, Bart., M.P. Demy 8vo. 1s.

**THE STATESMAN'S YEAR-BOOK: A Statistical** and Historical Annual of the States of the Civilised World, for the year 1881. By FREDERICK MARTIN. Eighteenth Annual Publication. Revised after Official Returns. Crown 8vo. 10s. 6d.

"The Statesman's Year-Book is the only work in the English language which furnishes a clear and concise account of the actual condition of all the States of Europe, the civilised countries of America, Asia, and Africa, and the British Colonies and Dependencies in all parts of the world.... of unimpeachable trustworthiness, such as no publication of the same kind has ever been able to furnish. As indispensable as Bradshaw."—TIMES.

**GUIDE to the STUDY of POLITICAL ECONOMY.** From the Italian of DR. LUIGI COSSA, Professor in the University of Pavia. With a Preface by W. STANLEY JEVONS, F.R.S. Crown 8vo. 4s. 6d.

## MACMILLAN AND CO., LONDON.

Now publishing, in Crown 8vo, price 2s. 6d. each.

# ENGLISH MEN OF LETTERS.

## Edited by JOHN MORLEY.

**JOHNSON.** By LESLIE STEPHEN. Crown 8vo. 2s. 6d.

"The new series opens well with Mr. Leslie Stephen's sketch of Dr. Johnson. It could hardly have been done better, and it will convey to the readers for whom it is intended a juster estimate of Johnson than either of the two essays of Lord Macaulay."—*Pall Mall Gazette.*

**SCOTT.** By R. H. HUTTON. Crown 8vo. 2s. 6d.

"We could not wish for a more suggestive introduction to Scott and his poems and novels."—*Examiner.*

**GIBBON.** By J. C. MORISON. Crown 8vo. 2s. 6d.

"As a clear, thoughtful, and attractive record of the life and works of the greatest among the world's historians, it deserves the highest praise."
—*Examiner.*

**SHELLEY.** By J. A. SYMONDS. Crown 8vo. 2s. 6d.

"The lovers of this great poet are to be congratulated at having at their command so fresh, clear, and intelligent a presentment of the subject, written by a man of adequate and wide culture."—*Athenæum.*

**HUME.** By Professor HUXLEY, F.R.S. Crown 8vo. 2s. 6d.

"It may fairly be said that no one now living could have expounded Hume with more sympathy or with equal perspicuity."—*Athenæum.*

**GOLDSMITH.** By WILLIAM BLACK. Crown 8vo. 2s. 6d.

"Mr. Black brings a fine sympathy and taste to bear in his criticism of Goldsmith's writings, as well as his sketch of the incidents of his life."—*Athenæum.*

**DEFOE.** By W. MINTO. Crown 8vo. 2s. 6d.

"Mr. Minto's book is careful and accurate in all that is stated, and faithful in all that it suggests. It will repay reading more than once."—*Athenæum.*

**BURNS.** By Principal SHAIRP. Crown 8vo. 2s. 6d.

"It is impossible to desire fairer criticism than Principal Shairp's on Burns' poetry. . . . None of the series has given a truer estimate either of character or of genius than this volume."—*Spectator.*

www.ingramcontent.com/pod-product-compliance
Lightning Source LLC
Chambersburg PA
CBHW021351230426
43666CB00006B/483